How To Analyze People

Secrets to Speed Reading People and Talk to Any Person. Dark Psychology, Manipulation and Mental Control.

Sophie Davies

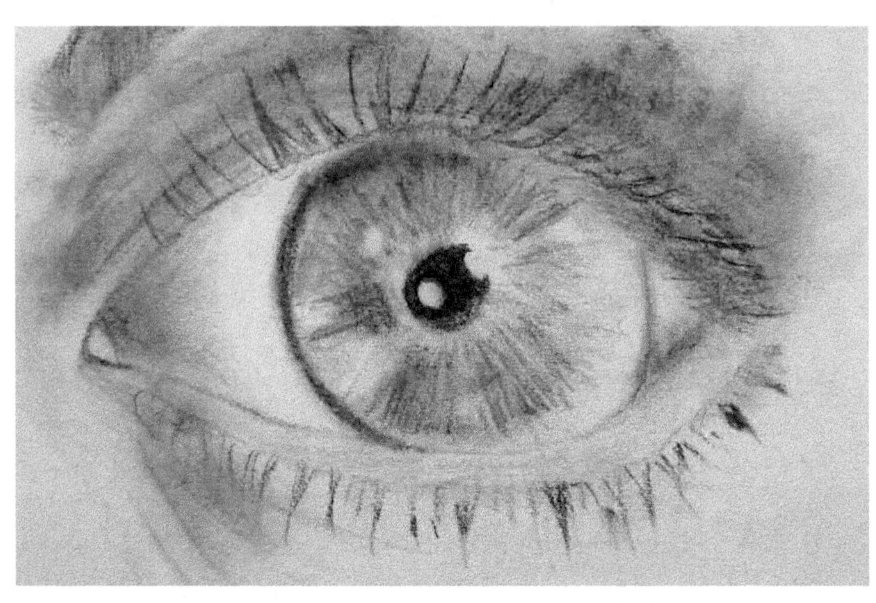

Table of Contents

INTRODUCTION

In our world today, we are surrounded by an abundance of information –
most often from corporations and companies promising us a quick fix for
whatever we may be struggling with or trying to achieve.

These offers tend to promise "the easy way out" and sometimes this is
exactly what you need. Whether it is something as simple as surviving
another day at work because your boss has nothing better to do than try
and bully you into quitting or finding that elusive crush at the office – there
are more positives than negatives in learning how to manipulate your inner
psychology to turn it against those who would use manipulation against
you.

The first thing to realize is that people who manipulate others are not
necessarily "bad". They have a different set of ethical beliefs than you
might, but it does not make them any less human, or any eviler. People are
constantly manipulating others around them. When you ask for something
at the grocery store, you are essentially manipulating the clerk into giving
you something for free or for a lower price than they should. When you
ask your boss for a raise, you are trying to manipulate your boss into
feeling bad about themselves so that you get what is rightfully yours.

The same goes for manipulation in relationships. The act of using
seduction is nothing but manipulation (albeit erotic manipulation). While
it can be a very effective tool to use in a relationship, when used in
conjunction with reason and a deep understanding of human psychology,
it can also be instrumental in the development of trust and love.

When using manipulation to get what you want out of people – you must
understand that they will try to use the same strategy on you, unless they
are completely clueless. If someone is doing something that they know is
frowned upon by society, that person will probably attempt to manipulate
other people into giving them something that is considered undesirable or
dangerous in exchange for their own "desired" items. This is not to say
that this person will be successful, but this is the kind of thinking that must
be understood. The ability to read and analyze people correctly is a useful
skill that can help you manoeuvre through life and making wise decisions.

If you master the skills to read someone by paying attention to the important things they do, which are, in most cases, involuntary actions – you can talk so much about them. You can reveal a part of them that the rest of the world is not aware of. You might not be a psychic or have the power to read minds and predict the future, but you can observe and will be surprised by what you find out about people.

Reading People Through Their Behaviour

Through behaviour, everyone manifests deep-seated and intrinsic thoughts and emotions in actions. You cannot give out what you do not have, although lots of people pretend to be what they are not. Over time, the reality tends to prevail because the truth can never be submerged for long. Most of the time, you can read and detect someone's real character and behaviour through a simple smile or laughter. You would be able to know when a person is faking a smile, like if your partner's eyes are not blinking when he or she is smiling with reversed lips. You could be suspicious of their behaviour.

You can still read about changes in someone's behaviour using the position of their arms when they are talking to you, like the folding of arms and crossing of legs could connote that they are at ease with you. Additionally, emotional traumas and psychological changes in a person could be observed by the pose of the hands and legs too.

Have you met with someone trying to control and influence you with his/her words? That is a sign of a person who desires power. You can predict someone's future actions and determine the motives behind his/her actions and decisions if you can carefully observe and read his/her behavioural trends and attitudes after a while.

Another way to read and decode a person's behaviour is by watching to see how they relate to others. Do they always try to mend broken fences between other people? Are they friendly and sociable? When a person exhibits these traits, you can infer that they have a kind and pleasant demeanour.

Reading an individual to understand the quality and standard of their personality is ideal. This will make you know what inspires them in setting achievable standards. Most of the time, they pride themselves on personal achievements instead of collaboration.

Reading People Through Their Body Language

Body language is one of the ways to read and analyze a person's attitudes and behaviours. Reading the movement of a person's eyes can determine the veracity of what one is saying. If the person is avoiding eye contact with your own eyes, scurrying his eyes on you, and staring at you for a long while, these are clues that he may be lying. Also, if your partner is not doing all these things, then he may be telling the truth.

You can read and detect when a person is not serious about your conversations if he/she is always reading messages on his phone and looking at their wristwatch. Paying rapt attention to their jobs instead of focusing on you is another sign that they are not connected with your discussions. Exhibiting these actions can also connote that they are bored with your speech and looking for ways to keep you away.

Allowing your intuition to register and decode the silent and subconscious expressions in a person's mind is one of the best ways to read that person like a book. Sometimes, it comes in a flash of light, but if you do not pick it immediately, you may miss it afterward.

How often does your crush or partner blink their eyes during a meeting? Constant blinking is a sign of uneasiness and jitteriness. Although in most cases, it is one of the features of attraction and seduction in a person. The human psychological analysis sees it is as a sign of anxiety, fear, and a higher influence for persuasion.

Reading a person's body language is akin to reading a book. Therefore, a quick gaze at a person can tell a lot about the individual. For instance, pursing lips denotes fear, anxiety, or surprise while clenched jaws suggest physical pressure and tensions.

You can know when your partner is stressed and strained if the individual is rubbing the fingers on the head and leaning away from you. Without mincing words, you should understand that when someone starts displaying these traits invariably, he is fatigued and perturbed.

Reading People Through Their Clothing or Appearance

'Appearance is deceitful' is a wise saying but reading people like a book cannot be overemphasized as another way of determining who a person is or telling about the job or profession an individual is engaged in through his/her appearance by the types of clothing he/she wears. For instance, if someone wears a suit you may say that they are a lawyer or banker, a lab coat suggests that one is a scientist, a uniform connotes military officer or police, overalls splattered by paint means a painter.

You can also tell a person's age through the lines and wrinkles on the face. Looking at the mouth, neck, and eyes, you will see some lines or wrinkles, and that will tell you that such a person is not too young.

If a person appears with faded clothes, you may conclude that such one is not too affluent, but an appearance on high-quality clothes, designer shoes, and bags, wristwatches, or even having a clean haircut or hairdo can suggest a show of affluence or a desire to be rich.

Furthermore, you can also observe if the individual is a choosy person through his appearance and dressing. Is the person dressed in well-pressed clothes, has a neat haircut, and pays more attention to their debut? Some individuals may choose to be more concerned and detail-oriented about their jobs rather than physical appearances.

Reading a person like a book will help you to know when to engage the person in small talk. Starting discussions in this way will make people open up themselves to chat with you.

FACIAL SIGNALS

The facial expression, along with the eyes, is one of the most important means to express emotions and moods.

Through knowledge and observation of facial expressions – that is, the moving face and not as a static object, we can get a better understanding of what others communicate to us.

We also make judgments about people's personalities and other traits based on what we see in their faces. For example, people with attractive features are often attributed certain qualities that they may or may not possess.

Although not all message communicated by facial expression is amendable to being consciously noticed by the interlocuter, it is well known that the undetectable movement of others' spoken communication influences our impressions of them.

The Face and First Impressions

In the first meeting between two people, the first five minutes are usually the most critical period. The impressions formed in this short space of time will tend to persist in the future. This can even be reinforced by subsequent behaviour, which is not usually interpreted objectively, but according to those first impressions.

Since the face is one of the first features we notice in a person, it can play a vital role in the process of establishing relationships with others.

In these few minutes, we form opinions about your character, personality, intelligence, temperament, ability to work, personal habits, and even about your convenience as a friend or lover.

Talking To the Face

Together with the eyes, the face is our best means to communicate without words. We use it – and the judgments of others will depend on the clues they get – to indicate how pleased we are as people, to express our current state of mind, to show the attention we pay to others, and so on. However, facial expressions can be used to reinforce the impact of verbal messages, such as when a mother scolds her child, the expression on her face will show if she is really angry.

The main function of the face in body language is the expression of emotions– although other parts of the body also contribute to the use we make of body language, so we should not believe that a message is clear and exclusively transmitted by a single part of the body.

The range of expressions is very wide, but there are a limited number of emotions that most of us can recognize with some reliability.

Paul Ekman and Wallace Friesen, have discovered that there are six main facial expressions:

Smiles

Smiles can be light, normal, and large. They are usually used as a gesture of greeting, to express varying degrees of pleasure, joy, and happiness. Even blind-born children smile when they like something. They are characterized by being beautiful and cheerful. Smiles can also be used to mask other emotions:

- Smile to hide the hardships. Smile as a submission response.
- Smile to make stressful situations more bearable. Smile to attract the smile of others.
- Smile to relax the tension. Smile to hide fear.

Sadness, Disappointment, And Depression

They are distinguished by lack of expression and by features such as the downward inclination of the corners of the mouth, low gaze, and general decay of the factions. Normally these emotions are accompanied by a low volume of the voice or a slower way of speaking.

Although in most cases they are not very well distinguished from each other, other bodily factors assure us of knowing which emotion is being carried out as:

Sadness

- Eyebrows slightly tilted towards the ears forming a semiarch. Shoulders regularly decayed.
- Inclination of the commissures at 45% of their normal range. Hands together and face down.

Disappointment

- Eyebrows not fully inclined.
- Looking back, and down, usually to the left.
- Shoulders slightly down and with the hands at the sides of the body.

Depression

- Normally inclined eyebrows.
- Tilt of the commissures slightly descending. Shoulders down.
- Legs and thighs parallel to each other.
- But we must remember that each emotion is different according to each individual. Not everyone demonstrates the same factions.

Dislike or Contempt

They express themselves with shrinkage of the eyes and puckering of the mouth. The nose is usually wrinkled, and the head is turned sideways to avoid having to look at the cause of such a reaction. It is the only facial expression that occurs in only part of the face, that is, in the middle of it. One end of the upper lip is lifted while the opposite side is in its original position.

Anger

Anger is often characterized by gazing into the cause of the offense, closed mouth and teeth tightly clenched, and eyes and eyebrows slightly inclined to express anger. Closed hands pressing and containing the feeling can also be seen in a situation of anger.

Fear

Fear is not a unique form of expression that reveals its presence. It can be revealed through very wide eyes, through the open mouth, or by a general tremor that affects the face and the rest of the body.

Interest

It is often detected by what is called a "bird's head", that is, the head tilts a certain angle towards the subject of interest. Other features are eyes more open than normal and mouth slightly open.

Another aspect to consider is the extent to which the complements in nonverbal messages are involved. Because the complements change our appearance, we must consider their effects on the perception that others have of us. From this, it can be deduced that we do not always transmit the nonverbal messages we try to send. The more aware we are of these difficulties of body language, without words, the better we can use it.

Other Information About the Face

Facial expressions, in addition to expressing emotions, also serve as a means of expressing personality, attitudes towards others, sexual attraction and attractiveness, the desire to communicate or initiate an interaction, and the degree of expressiveness during communication.

Women tend to laugh and smile more often than men, which does not have to be due to greater sociability or joy. It may be because they find the situation slightly uncomfortable.

The expression of the face is constantly changing during communication. Among the changes, we can mention the so-called "micro-momentary" facial expressions. As its name indicates, its duration is a fraction of a second and usually reflects the true feelings of a person.

Laughter

Laughter is a response biological produced by the body in response to certain stimuli. The smile is considered a soft and silent form of laughter. There are currently various interpretations about its nature.

The most recent studies, high impact, are made since 1999 by Robert Provine, a neurobiologist of the behaviour of the University of Maryland, who said laughter is a "babbling playful, instinctive, contagious, stereotyped and control unconscious, or involuntary – which rarely occurs in solitude". In humans, laughter begins, on average, towards four months of age, and, according to recent scientific studies, it constitutes a form of innate communication inherited from primates and closely related to language.

On the other hand, for other authors, such as Charles R. Gruner, of the University of Georgia (1978), laughter is reminiscent or synonymous with the shout of triumph of the fighter after winning his adversary. Ensures that in all manifestations of humour there is a gesture of aggression, even in the most innocuous cases. According to Gruner, "even an infant laugh, not as a manifestation of thanks, but because he got what he wanted". The philosopher John Morreall (1983) argues that the biological origin of human laughter could be in a shared expression of relief after passing the danger – the laxity we feel after laughing can help inhibit the aggressive response, turning laughter into a sign of behaviour that indicates trust in classmates.

In any case, there is recent research conducted both in orangutans and chimpanzees that suggest that they can laugh, which would make laughter of evolutionary and genetic origin.

It is popularly considered a response to moments or situations of humor, as an external expression of fun, related to joy and happiness. Although laughter, according to numerous studies, such as Robert Provine, is motivated by a comic stimulus in a minority of everyday cases. It usually appears, more or less simulated, as an emotional complement to verbal messages, as well as in situations of stress or playful behaviours such as tickling.

Some medical theories attribute beneficial effects on health and well-being to laughter since it releases endorphins.

Forms Of Laughter

Depending on the force with which it occurs, laughter can vary both in its duration and in its tone and characteristics. Thus, we use different words to describe what we consider different types of laughter such as click, laugh, giggle, contemptuous, desperate, nervous, and equivocal laughter. Other types include coquina, jingle, evil laugh, and hypoid.

Among the emotional cues, the smile is the most contagious of all, and smiling encourages positive feelings. Like the laugh itself, the smile is innate, and deaf and blind children smile. It usually appears at six weeks of life and is the first language of the human being. Initially, it is a physical behaviour and gradually evolves into an emotional one. Self-induction of the gesture of smiling can improve our mood. Another property is to induce an increase in the activity of NK cells and thus improve our immune status.

Some studies show that laughter varies by gender – women tend to laugh in a more singing way, while men tend to laugh snorting or growling.

Physiology Of Laughter

It occurs when a stimulus – internal or external – is processed in primary, secondary, and multimodal association areas of the central nervous system. The processing of emotions is carried out in the limbic system, which is probably responsible for the potential motors that characterize laughter, including facial expression and the movements of the muscles that control ventilation and phonation. Once the stimulus has been processed, in addition to the aforementioned automatic motor acts, a generalized autonomous activation is carried out, which has an exit through several routes, among which are the hypothalamus-pituitary axis and the autonomic nervous system. All these components make up the emotion, a process that involves, when it comes to joy, the motor act called laughter.

There are two structures of the limbic system involved in the production of laughter – the amygdala and the hippocampus.

Some Studies

Laughter can be induced by stimulating the subthalamic nucleus. It has been proven in patients with Parkinson's disease. Recent work by Itzhak Fried et al., from the University of California, has allowed us to locate an area of the brain called a supplementary motor area, which, when stimulated using electrodes, produces the smile and with more intense stimulation, laughing out loud. The supplementary motor area is an area very close to the language area. This mechanism was discovered accidentally while treating a young woman with epilepsy.

Experiments have been conducted to determine exactly in which area the sense of humour resides. In a study, presented in 2000 by scientists at the University of Rochester, volunteers underwent functional magnetic resonance while asking them various questions. They concluded that this characteristic resided in a small region of the frontal lobe. However, another London team performed the same test on individuals who were told jokes, and the results were that the brain area that was activated was the ventral prefrontal cortex along with other regions involved in the language process when the joke's grace resided in a pun.

Medical Perspective

Every day we laugh less. Children 7-10 years laugh around 300 times a day, while adults who still laugh do less than 80 times a day. Some people rarely laugh, and some do not even feel the need to laugh.

Studies since the 1980s by the Psychoneuroimmunology Lee S. Berk and colleagues demonstrated over several years the positive effects of laughter:

Some stress-related indicators decreased during laughter episodes, related to decreased epinephrine and cortisone levels.

The laughter increased the production of antibodies and the activation of protective cells such as lymphocytes or cytotoxic T lymphocytes, which produce cellular immunity, important to prevent the formation of tumours.

Cheerful and repetitive laughter or laughter improved mood reduced blood cholesterol levels and regulated blood pressure.

More recently in 2010, Berk has discovered a relationship between laughter and appetite. It was seen that laughter increases appetite analogously to how moderate physical exercise does. According to these studies, there is simultaneously a reduction in the level of leptin and an increase in ghrelin in the blood.

Other beneficial effects of laughter are as follows: Free from fear and anguish.

- It helps to calm the anger.
- It contributes to a change of mental attitude that favors the decrease of diseases.
- It promotes digestion by increasing the contractions of all abdominal muscles.
- It facilitates the evacuation due to the "massage" that it produces on the viscera.
- It increases the heart rate and pulse and, by stimulating the release of "endorphin" hormones, allows them to fulfill one of their important functions, such as maintaining the elasticity of the coronary arteries.
- It decreases the presence of cholesterol in the blood as it amounts to aerobic exercise.
- It helps reduce blood glucose.

HANDS

The hands come with twenty-seven bones each and are an expressive aspect of our body. They offer us huge capabilities as an advanced species in the way we deal with our surroundings. After the face, the hands are perhaps the best source of body language.

It should be noted that hand gestures vary significantly across cultures and what you deem a normal hand signal in your country could result in you getting arrested in another.

A hand signal could be minor, perhaps trying to betray your subconscious thoughts. It may also be done using both hands while trying to stress a point.

Major Hand Cues

The following are some of the major hand cues in body language:

Holding

Cupped hands create a container that can hold something softly. Gripped hands can hold something tightly. Hands can hold together or individually. Cupped hands can signify a fragile idea.

They can also be utilized for giving.

- Holding oneself can equally be an act of restraint. It can be to allow the other individual to speak. It can also be utilized when the individual is mad, efficiently preventing them from violence.
- The tension of a holding group shows the amount of pressure the individual feels. Folded arms could be relaxed. However, if the hands are holding the opposite arms, it becomes more preventive.
- Holding hands behind you leaves the front open and can display confidence. Hidden hands may also display tension. When a hand holds the other arm, the tighter the grip and higher the hold determine how great the tension is.

- Both hands can display varying desires. For example, one hand creating a fist and the other holding it back shows restraint from punching someone or something else.

Also, individuals who are being deceptive often try to keep their hands in check. You may get suspicious when they remain still with one often holding the other. Another signal could be holding them behind. These are only likely signals, and you should also watch out for related signs.

Control

A hand with the palm facing downward may restrain or hold the other person figuratively. It could be an act of authority like, "Stop this instantly!" It could also be a request like, "Please hold on." This also comes up in the leading hand on a top handshake. Palms downward while inclined on a desk usually show dominance.

- An outward-facing palm toward others pushes them away or fends them off in a less subtle method than the palms-down sign.
- A pointing hand or finger informs an individual where to head.

Hiding

Individuals may hide their hands by placing them in pockets, behind their back, underneath their legs or the table. Hands are frequently used in communication and the hiding of hands may signal a yearning not to collaborate or communicate. They may be saying, "I don't agree with you" or "I don't want to speak to you."

- Individuals may hide their hands as a deliberate sign of disobedience, like putting their hands in their pockets. Liars may keep their hands hidden out of worry that they may expose themselves.
- Hiding hands may also be a way of listening, passing across the message, "I want to listen, not talk."
- Placing hands behind the back or in pockets can also be due to a feeling of relaxation and not wanting to speak.

Finger Signals

Fingers are quite flexible and support subtle signals. Below are a few of these:

Pointer

- A pointing finger signifies direction. For lengthy distances, individuals could point the finger upward in a diagonal manner like shooting an arrow.
- Pointing at others is similar to prodding and is mostly classified as threatening and rude.
- Individuals who are mad tend to point more. This pointing includes at themselves when they feel insulted or hurt and at those, they feel are responsible.

Prod

Rudeness

- Prodding can function like a stiletto knife, piercing forward at the other individual. The index finger is typically used, but sometimes the middle finger is utilized. Prodding is usually threatening and taken as a personal attack.
- The prod can also be used in pointing downward at an item that is not there. It is not as menacing as pointing straight at an individual.
- The middle finger pointing up implies a swear and signifies a penis. In this gesture, the little finger suggests that the other individual has a tiny penis. It is sometimes utilized as a rude sign from a lady to a man.
- The initial two fingers pointing upward while the palm faces toward oneself implies f**k off. On the other hand, the palm facing the other individual connotes peace.

Thumbs-up

- Thumbs-up shows agreement and approval. Thumbs-down shows a lack of consent. When held sideways, it implies uncertainty.

- Thumbs-up when crossing arms or a single handheld across the chest is a subtle approval sign. It can also be a way of inviting others to show that they approve of what you are saying.
- Thumbs that stick out when you place your hands in your pocket are usually an indication of confidence, feeling in control, and relaxed. For this reason, the gesture could be a sign of friendliness and authority.
- In a few cultures, giving a thumbs-up implies sexual interest. In other cultures, it might just be rude.

Other Signals

- Crossed fingers show hope.
- Inspection of fingernails portrays disinterest and boredom. Fingers fluttering may portray uncertainty.
- Fidgeting fingers may show tension or boredom.
- Sucking of fingers is a relapse to breastfeeding and childhood. It may also portray feelings of inferiority and timidity.

Basic Interpretations of Handshakes and Hand Gestures

Similar to the way a person writes, the way they shake hands offers a clue to their inner nature. So, if you are aware of what every handshake says about the people with whom you are interacting, you can make good use of this information.

Below are a few kinds of handshakes and what they mean:

Dominance

Dominance is displayed with one hand placed above the other, extended holding, and holding the individual using the other hand.

Affection

Affection is displayed with the duration and speed of the shake, touching using the other hand, and smiling enthusiastically. Affectionate and dominant handshakes are similar and may result in a confusing situation where a dominant individual acts friendly.

Submission

Submission is displayed with a floppy hand, palm up (which may be clammy at times), and a fast withdrawal.

Kinds of Handshakes

Dead Fish

This form of handshake has no energy, no squeeze, no shake, and no pinch. It makes you feel as if you are holding a dead fish as opposed to a hand. This handshake is associated with low self-esteem.

Sweaty Palms

When a person is anxious, their nervous system often gets overactive, which in turn leads to sweaty palms.

The Two-handed Handshake

This handshake is typically common with politicians. It is a form of handshake that brings to mind words like "friendly," "trustworthy," "warmth," and "honest." If the hand remains on your hand, the handshake is sincere. But if the hand moves to your arms, wrists, or elbows, they want something from you.

Brush off

This kind of handshake is a fast grasp then a release that seems as if your hand is being pushed aside. The handshake implies that your agenda is not essential.

Controller

If you feel the other person pulling your hand toward him or directing it to another direction or a chair, this kind of person is a controller. It implies that they need to be in control of both animate and inanimate items in the room, including you.

Bone Crusher

This kind of handshake, which has to do with squeezing your hands until you begin cringing, aims to intimidate you. For these individuals, you do not need to pretend to be weak. They might even respond positively if you display your strength.

Finger Vice

When a person grips your fingers as opposed to your whole hand, the aim is to keep you far from them. These individuals are usually secure. If they crush your fingers, they are including a display of personal power aimed to hold you at a distance.

The Top-Handed Shake

As opposed to holding his hand vertically, this shaker does so horizontally so his hand is above yours. This gesture implies he feels he is superior to you.

Lobster Claw

Similar to a lobster claw, the other individual's fingers and thumb touch your palm. This individual is scared of deep connections and may have issues in developing relationships. Give them time and let them open up when they want.

The Pusher

While this individual gives you a handshake, she stretches her arms, so you are unable to get close. This kind of individual requires space and is not allowing you in. You must provide them the emotional and physical space they want if you plan on building a friendship with them.

LEGS

Here is a question for you – "Which part of the body do you think will give you an accurate read on a person's true intentions?" Most people will unequivocally point to the face. Well, they are wrong.

Research shows that the legs are the most honest part of our body. It is a fact that the further away a body part is from the brain, the less awareness we have of what it is doing.

Early in life, we are taught to always put on a brave face, smile, and bear the pain. Perhaps we were taught to smile and show appreciation when our grandma gives us that ugly sweater for Christmas. No offense, Grandma. It is no surprise that we learned to be good at hiding our facial expressions as we grew up.

However, we never learned how to mask our emotions through our legs, and that is why it is not easy to fake our leg movements. For instance, a person can look composed and put on their best poker face while their foot is repeatedly tapping the ground, revealing their frustration at not being able to leave.

Why Are the Legs Accurate Reflections of Our Emotional State?

It all boils down to evolution. Ever since the early men started walking upright, our legs have helped us to run, kick, swivel, jump, and do many activities. Our legs have helped us to serve two main purposes – run away from danger and move forward to get food. In other words, our legs are hardwired to go after what we want and move away from what we do not want.

The legs show a person's willingness to stay in a conversation or leave. Leg movements are noticeable in children since they have an unbridled emotional state. Let us take a look at one of the basic scenarios of how the legs betray our emotional state.

A few years ago, there was a poker tournament on TV. I saw this guy deal a powerful hand. Underneath the table, his feet were bouncing and wiggling like a little child going on a vacation. Above the table, he put on a stoic "poker face." The other players who could not see the excited movements of his legs under the table called his bet and lost their money to him.

We often do not pay attention to the feet when observing others. What we fail to realize is emotion is revealed through our leg movements.

From the stance of an angry person to the shy feet of a child meeting strangers to the nervous pacing of a father as he waits in the delivery room, all these signals reveal our emotional state and help us to observe them in others.

So, if you want to decode the world around you, watch the feet of others. Let us examine the significant nonverbal signals of the feet and legs.

Excited Feet Displays

An example of this is a poker tournament where one of the players was able to mask his facial expression yet could not stop the wiggling and bouncing off his legs in excitement. This nonverbal gesture can be called the excited feet display.

People display this leg movement when they have heard or seen something that positively affects them. It is a solid signal that the person feels he is in an advantageous position to get what he wants from the other person.

So how can you detect an excited foot since it is inappropriate for you to look under the table? Before I answer that, it is paramount to know that not every excited foot display represents excitement or happiness.

Sometimes, it is a sign of nervousness or impatience. It is a sign of happiness or excitement if the intensity of the leg movements increases after the person hears positive news.

The Leg-Shift Display

We turn toward things we like and find agreeable and move away from things we find disagreeable. You can use this information to see whether others are happy to see you or not.

Here is a simple test to carry out – walk toward two people engaged in a conversation. Mind you, ensure these are individuals you have met before. So, walk up to them and say, "Hi." At this moment, you are not sure if they want your company. How can you know their true feelings toward your company? By examining their feet and body behaviour.

If they move their torso along with their feet to face you, then your company is welcome. Though, if they only swivel their hips to say hello without pointing their feet toward you, then they would rather be left alone.

This behaviour is also important in conversations. When a person turns his feet away from you toward the exit, it is a sign of disengagement, a desire to move away from the conversation. When someone shifts their feet away from you, it can be a sign that the person does not want to be around you anymore. Perhaps you might have said something annoying or disagreeable.

The Knee-Clasp Display

This is also another leg movement that shows someone is ready to leave or end the conversation. It is a sitting position that involves a forward lean of the torso followed by placing both hands on the knee in a knee clasp. When you see this display in someone, it is a sign that they are ready to conclude the meeting and leave. Always take note of this cue, especially when it is coming from a superior.

The Gravity-Defying Leg Display

We have examined the nonverbal cues people give off when they do not want to stay around you. How can we use the nonverbal signals of the legs to detect when someone is excited to see us? I'm sure you probably think it is easy to detect that. Well, let me ask you a question – what if the person does not want you to know how excited he is about seeing you or about a prospect?

Some people do not always show it in their facial features when they are excited to see you. Rather, they exhibit certain gravity-defying leg gestures that reveal their true intentions. These gravity-defying feature includes rocking up and down the balls of your feet. Sometimes, it includes walking with a spring in your step.

They might point their toes skyward while the heel of the foot remains on the ground.

Here is an interesting note – people with clinical depression rarely exhibit this nonverbal clue.

Territorial Leg Displays

Before we discuss the leg display gesture and other types of dominant leg displays, I believe we need to understand the importance of personal space. We need to know why the more assured or superior we think we are, the more territory we tend to claim for ourselves.

This leads us to the work of Edward Hall, who studied the importance of personal space in humans and animals. He discovered that the more personal space one demanded, the more self-confident and assured the person is of their status. Therefore, CEOs and higher-ups can claim greater space for themselves.

For the rest of us, we are very protective of our personal space, and we do not like it when people stand too close. The brain releases negative limbic reactions when someone invades your personal space. So, keep this in mind when someone stands too close to you or vice versa.

The Leg-Splay Territorial Display

The leg splay is one of the most unmistakable and easily spotted dominant leg behaviours. People become territorial when they feel threatened or when they want to threaten others. This leg behaviour involves spreading your legs far apart as a way of showing masculinity and authority. It is no surprise that law enforcement officers assume this position a lot in the presence of criminals and other officers.

The leg-splay behaviour sends a strong message to the astute observer that there are issues to solve or there is a potential for trouble.

Defensive-Leg Displays

Crossed-Leg Display

We are going to examine the importance of the crossed-leg position and how it complements the crossed-arm position in giving off a defensive front. Here is an example to better illustrate this defensive position.

There was a conference involving two groups of people, group A and group B, having contrasting opinions about a matter. When a representative from group A took the stage to address the issue, all the people in group B, as if controlled by a puppet, assumed the crossed-arm and crossed-leg positions. By unconsciously doing this, group B was not buying into what the speaker from the other group was saying.

Therefore, if you are trying to persuade someone who assumes this leg position, you have to get them to uncross. You can achieve this by inviting them to sit beside you or give them something to hold like a brochure.

The Ankle Lock

This is a favorite position most people assume when they are in a dental seat, waiting for the dentist to get the work done. Most people also take this position at the start of an interview. Why? This leg behaviour stems from fear, guilt, and uncertainty. Generally, the ankle-lock position means crossing your legs at the ankle.

In males, there is usually a clenched fist resting on the knees or hands tightly gripping the arms of a chair.

The female version is a bit different. The knees are held together, and the arms are gently placed side by side on the legs. Most times, this gesture reveals that the person is holding back a negative emotion, such as fear or uncertainty. Interviewees also assume this position when they are uncomfortable. To break the "ice" and get them to open up, you need to make them relax and break the ankle lock.

Sometimes, people might take the ankle lock a bit further, and this time around, they lock their ankles around the chair while gripping the armrest of a chair tightly. This behaviour reveals that something is troubling the person. In this case, you can also look out for clusters that reveal the same emotion as the ankle lock. For instance, an individual who locks his ankle around the chair is likely to move his hands along his legs as a pacifying behaviour.

An individual might move their feet from the front of the chair to under the chair. This withdrawing signal is an indication of rising stress levels. Over the years, I have concluded that people will often withdraw their feet underneath the chair when a high-stress question is asked. To the observant investigator or interviewer, this is a sign that the question evokes discomfort in the respondent, and they can decide to press further toward that line of inquiry. As the subject changes, the person will gradually withdraw the feet from underneath the chair in response to the limbic brain's relief that the question is changed.

When utilized properly, these nonverbal cues can help you get a better read on people in all manner of settings. When you merge your knowledge of the nonverbals of the legs and feet with signals from other parts of the body, then you become adept at understanding what people are feeling and thinking, and you can guess their next course of action. Therefore, let us turn our attention to the nonverbal signals of the hands and feet.

OTHER BODY LANGUAGE CUES

Aside from the specific gestures and particular body movements, you also want to start creating a baseline that helps you analyze the cues the body is communicating as a whole. There is always general non-verbal communication being transmitted when you observe a person. For example, you might notice how animated, edgy, calm, poised, or stoic the person in front of you might appear. He or she might be expressing a sense of vibrant energy and seem very upbeat and happy, or they might be cumbersome and dull. In this chapter, we want to address some of the more prominent body movements and what they indicate to help you read people more accurately.

The Chest

Chest protrusion can be considered a sexual or aggressive body language posture. Men do it to appear more dominant, which is meant to repel other aggressive men and attract members of the opposite sex. When women do it, they usually want to draw attention to their breasts, making them appear large so they can attract the attention of men.

Chest puffing occurs when a person inhales deeply and expands the lungs, so they appear larger and more dominant. Mostly a very male body posture. You can read this as a sign of conflict arising. Often when a guy does this, he also arches his back and holds his head up in an exaggerated form to amplify the puffed-up chest.

The Shoulder

Shoulder embrace usually occurs between adult men or between mother and her child and is generally non-sexual. Read it as a non- verbal sign of affection where the arms are put around another's shoulder.

Shoulder shrugs or a shoulder rise are usually an expression of uncertainty or doubt. You can read it as a sign of indifference, resignation, helplessness, or even ignorance depending on the context. The person will move his or her shoulders upward toward the ears.

The Hips

The hip tilt is a female move. A woman will slouch to one side forcing her hips to emphasize her curves. It is a simple way of drawing attention to her genitals. In the fashion world, you see it a lot, and perhaps the more exaggerated version known as the catwalk is all meant to draw the eye to the beaconing genital region.

Hip embrace is when two people (usual lovers) walk side by side with their arms around the hips of the other. Read it as a sharp display of intimacy.

The Torso

Torso shield is when a person uses their arm or an object to shield their chest area to protect it from a perceived threat. This can be subtle in the form of holding a drink across the body, playing with their tie or cufflink, or it can be more obvious as a full arm cross.

Read it as an expression that the other person is protecting himself or herself from something, and they have a difference of opinion.

Torso splay is a dominant body posture in which the person lies back in a comfortable position with the chest puffed out and open, almost challenging an attack. Read it as a sign of high comfort and the person communicating to you that they feel in charge of the situation.

Expressing Yourself with Body Posture

Did you know that you express yourself daily using your body posture? Posture is the way you hold your body during movement and while at rest. There are two main types of body posture that you need to become aware of. Dynamic and static body posture. Let us take a closer look at each.

Dynamic Posture

It refers to how the body is aligned during activity or movement. Generally, this involves moving the whole body in a particular way. With dynamic posture, we want to make sure we move lightly, and the knees are slightly bent, the senses and mind are engaged, etc. Movement such as walking, running, jumping, dancing, and so on are all forms of dynamic posture. Our bodies are highly adaptable, and they are ever looking for the path of least resistance, which is why poor posture is terrible because it inevitably becomes the default setting, which eventually leads to decreased flexibility, performance, and lots of unnecessary aches.

Static Posture

Static posture refers to how your body is aligned when stationary or when standing. Spend the next week observing how you stand. Keep a mirror in all the rooms where you frequently stand so you can see yourself. Are your shoulders rounded, level, or elevated? What about your head? Do your knees track over the second and third toes? You want to make sure your body can hold itself up with the least amount of energy yet maintaining proper form.

The key to good posture, whether it is dynamic or static, is the position of your spine. There are three natural curves you want to become more familiar with. These are the neck, the mid-back, and the low back curve. Good posture is about maintaining these curves, not increasing or decreasing them. How can you do this? Make sure your head is always above your shoulders, and

the top of your shoulder is over your hips. In our modern society, given the fact that we spend so much time sitting behind a desk or typing on a computer, you need to keep doing some check-ins throughout the day to ensure you are maintaining good posture. If you carry around heavy bags or lift heavy things often, then you also need to keep reinforcing the right alignment because these activities often through off our alignment.

The Two Forms of Non-Verbal Posture

When reading body language, either your own or another person's, the two primary signals you might receive are open or closed. Open means the person is not defensive and is more willing and open to interacting. The closed posture means the opposite, of course. To a certain degree, the posture form you read in a person can tell you how confident they are and how receptive they are likely to be if you interacted. For example, imagine walking up to two strangers, both sitting at a table because you needed directions to the bathroom. One had their arms crossed, and he was hunched over while the other sat with an open chest, head level, shoulders, and faced relaxed. Who would you talk to first?

Anytime you interact with someone or if you are about to interact with a person, take a moment to read the form they have. They will either be transmitting a closed or open posture.

Closed Posture

Whether the trunk of the body is left open and exposed. That usually indicates the person is very open to interacting and friendly.

Open Posture

Where the trunk of the body is hidden in the form of crossing arms and legs or hunching forward. That usually means the person is not that friendly, is not willing to engage, and might be anxious or even hostile.

Notice how much easier it feels to walk up and interact with people who carry themselves in an open posture. Most of the "cool guys" tend to carry themselves in a way that makes them look "open" like you need to be around them. Observe how many people around you, especially the ones you like are communicating this form of posture. Even when you want to approach someone you feel attracted to, it will be more comforting, and you will have more confidence when the person looks open instead of closed. Now that you have this awareness, pay more attention to the form of non-verbal posture, you transmit when interacting with others in social settings.

TIPS FOR SPEED-READING PEOPLE

Speed reading is a technique that seeks to increase the reading speed without compromising understanding and retention of information. There are several different speed-reading methods for both books and online texts, and they all aim to read as well as faster.

Check out this step-by-step guide and learn how to enhance your speed-reading skills!

Train Your Eyes to Make Bigger Jumps

Do you know how the movement of your eyes works while reading? It is a jumping move. Your eyes pin one point on the line and then jump to the next.

The higher this leap, the more proficient is your reading. Beginner readers, like children, skip only one word at a time and therefore take longer to finish each line. Therefore, the first step of speed reading is to train eye movement so that it is wider.

Go Straight Ahead

The second step is to control that anxiety, that sense of obligation to understand 100% of the text. We are going to take this up further but know that 80% understanding is an excellent goal.

After all, re-reading can take a long time – and that is precisely what we are trying to avoid.

In addition, you can fully understand the general idea of a text, even though some excerpts are more confusing. Then, after finishing the text, resume only the parts where you have doubts. But if you stop and go back constantly, you will never finish reading.

Another important tip is to not interrupt the reading to check the dictionary. If you are very curious about the meaning of a word, write it down to check later. However, do not abandon the text to browse the dictionary because when you return, it will take you even longer to resume reading.

In the meantime, try to understand the term by context – you may not absorb the exact meaning of the word, but it will be enough to understand the message the author wanted to convey.

Stop Speaking the Words

The third step is to eliminate a negative practice that is a habit of many people such as pronouncing the words as they read, either loudly or mentally.

This habit prevents the development of speed reading because it means that you will read word for word.

The speed slows down and as incredible as it may seem, the capacity for understanding as well. Because your brain will be busy with pronunciation, you will not be able to concentrate on interpreting what you are reading. The result is that you will have to reread the same stretch several times.

If you are too accustomed to pronouncing as you read, losing this habit can be a difficult and time-consuming process. An interesting tip is to put a pencil in your mouth as you read. With a little practice, you will lose this "craze" and see how it improves your reading time.

Use Skimming Technique

The fourth step is "skimming." This is a well-known technique for Instrumental English, but it is also useful for speed reading in any language.

Skimming consists basically of looking quickly through a text to extract basic information – index, title, author, date of publication, main subject, subtopics developed, graphics and images.

This technique is useful for you to quickly evaluate any text and then set whether to devote more time to a full reading.

If you are researching on a specific subject, for example, skimming will allow you to identify whether a particular article or book has relevant information about the subject. In addition, you will find the excerpts that interest you more easily.

Use The Scanning Technique

The fifth step, "scanning," is another technique used in English Instrumental. It consists basically of looking at the text to identify keywords, which in this case are relevant terms, related to the information you want to extract from that content.

Suppose you are reading a twenty-page article on People Management, but the subject that matters to you is Productivity. In that case, you do not have to read all twenty pages – which will certainly tell you about various other issues that are not important to you right now.

Instead, just look through the article for terms directly related to productivity, such as "time," "organization," "concentration," and so on. When you find one of these terms, you just need to read that passage. Thus, you quickly get information that is of interest to you and "skip" the rest.

Monitor Your Performance

Once you incorporate what you have learned in the first five steps, the evolution of your speed reading will depend on practice. But to see if it is working, you need to keep track of your progress.

So, the sixth step is picking up a timer and monitoring how many words you read per minute. As a reference, keep in mind that a typical reader reads, on average, 150 words per minute. Meanwhile, a good speed-reading practitioner can read up to 800 words per minute.

But do not just monitor speed. Consider, also, the use of reading, that is, how much you can understand the text without having to return to it a second time. Your goal should be an average of 80% utilization.

Remember that there is no point in speeding up reading, and thereby lessening the understanding of what has been read, as the re-reading also represents a waste of time.

Train Your Focusing Ability

Now that we have covered the best strategies for speed reading itself, let us take a few tips that will enhance your reading experience as a whole and as a result, help you absorb more information in less time.

The ability to stay focused while reading is critical to being productive and not wasting time. The deeper you "plunge" into the text, the better you understand what the author wrote.

What happens, then, if you go to every two paragraphs to check the notifications on your cell phone? The experience will be interrupted and continually resumed, which diminishes your ability to comprehend and thus takes you to take more time to understand what is read.

In this way, you waste twice as much time – the extra time it takes to understand what you read, and the precious minutes wasted with distractions such as smartphones, computers, social networks, etc.

If you often suffer from it, the key is to turn productivity into a habit. To do so, when you read, keep the distractions away. This means not leaving the phone nearby, not keeping the computer by your side, and, if possible, turning off the internet or at least placing your devices in airplane mode.

This time is for you to dedicate to the text and nothing else! The more you can focus on reading, the better your ability to practice speed reading.

Find A Quiet Place to Do Your Reading

The place you choose to do your readings also greatly influences the speed and dynamism of the activity – something very connected to the danger represented by the distractions, as we just mentioned.

Noise from traffic, from work, from an establishment – such as a bar, and even from music can disturb your ability to concentrate, making you frequently "quit" reading. Also, if you are reading in an environment with other people, you will be directly interrupted if they speak to you, even if it is a quick dialogue.

Aside from being silent, it is also important that the chosen corner for reading is comfortable. When you are comfortable reading, it is much easier to indulge in the text and devote your full attention to it. And if you have a special space where you like to read, another advantage is that this will make it easier to establish reading as an integral part of your routine.

Do Not Insist When You Are Tired

You may have heard that it is not very productive for a student to spend the night studying for a test that will be given the next day. At that point, the desperation of a few extra hours of study is no longer as important as the rest, which will allow more focus and better memory for the student during the test.

When we are tired, regardless of whether the exhaustion reaches our site and/or head, our ability to concentrate decreases dramatically. You will find yourself having to read and reread the same passage several times, and of course, it takes much longer to read each line.

And the worst part is that the next day you can pick up the text and realize you cannot remember much of anything you read the night before. This is because a tired brain also decreases its ability to retain information.

So, an important point of speed reading is to know the time to stop.

Read Whenever You Can

What the reader does not like to sit in their favorite armchair and deliver hours and hours to a book or even a relevant and high-quality text? However, as you well know, this is not always (or rather, rarely!) possible.

Does this mean, then, that you are bound to a routine? Of course not! It turns out you do not have to self-punch yourself for not being able to devote several hours of each day to reading.

Start enjoying every free minute, especially with regards to idle time spent in queues, waiting rooms, or on public transportation, for example. And how about going a little early to bed, every night, and reading before bed?

A block of fifteen or twenty minutes in which you would do nothing when dedicated to reading becomes time well spent. With this, you advance much faster in your readings, although you cannot read much each day. Another advantage is that this will help you build the daily habit of reading - and, who knows, it will even encourage you to separate a few hours of your day into the activity.

Do you already practice speed reading? What are your speed and reading achievement? If you have not yet reached the goals proposed here, do not worry. Reading is a habit you cannot be afraid to develop, and the benefits are gigantic.

Keep in mind, however, that the tendency is to improve your vocabulary with constant reading. And with a complete vocabulary, you will have more and more facilities to read and understand longer texts.

Essential Tips You Should Know About Speed Reading

Learn how to read more quickly by ensuring that all the content you learn is not lost in your mind after a few days.

Answer quickly! Do you read fast or slow? Have you ever tried to calculate your reading speed? By chance, have you heard of dynamic reading?

If not, you should. Well, if you love reading or even depending on it for studies, this advanced reading mode could help you a lot!

Dynamic reading is a faster type of reading which makes you read a lot in a short time. You may be thinking – reading fast is easy, but you cannot memorize it that way. Therefore, dynamic reading ensures this without impairing its ability to absorb content.

We have prepared some essential tips for you to start increasing your reading speed.

Understand that there are different types of reading speed. There are some reading differences that you may not know about, and it is important to know. As we said, a more agile and concentrated reading reduces the time needed for learning. Therefore, it optimizes productivity and ensures that all content learned is not lost in your mind after a few days.

This is essential for students, contestants, or even law and medical market professionals who need to read constantly. But this is not restricted to a group of people. Dynamic reading can help someone who already has a habit of reading to make you a reader with an even greater repertoire.

It must be understood that dynamic reading has two fundamental factors. These include content speed and retention. In short, reading too slowly can hinder the progress of any reading, or study. Just like reading too fast and not understanding the subject is not good either.

Therefore, it is essential to find a balance by reading at a fast speed that does not detract from the retention of information.

Valuable tips for anyone who wants to start dynamic reading!

- Start slowly. Read every 15 minutes free!
- Subtract only minutes from your daily activities to read.
- Walk around with a book in hand and use short spaces of time to read.
- Read for 20 minutes while waiting for dinner to be ready in the oven.
- Read while waiting for the bus to work and if possible, even within driving.

- With time and practice, dynamic reading will already be in your effortlessly!

HOW TO BE A BETTER READER?

Reading other people is not all about what you can do for yourself. It is also about what you can do for other people. You will learn how to set people at their ease, tell when they need something that they cannot or would not tell you about, and, perhaps most importantly, how to understand them and their needs, hopes, and desires. There is no greater gift you can offer to another human being than understanding and accepting of who they are and willing to provide what they are looking for.

Free Your Judgment

Many things can cloud your judgment when reading people. Biases, intimidation, and sexual attraction are just some of the things that can make you choose to ignore your gut and misread someone. You may think that someone's harsh actions are admirable if you admire the person, while their actions would appear despicable if you did not admire them. Do not let anything cloud your judgment.

Men are more likely to judge pretty young women less harshly. They let pretty young women get away with disrespectful behaviour in hopes of winning their favor. If you are attracted to someone, you are more likely to ignore red flags about the person. Try to look past sexual attraction. Understand that there are plenty of attractive people in the world, so fixating on one person's attractiveness is not necessary. You just need to view an attractive person more objectively. Try to focus on his or her character as a separate thing from his or her looks.

Status or certain jobs can also make you admire someone. But understand that someone is not perfect just because of his or her status. Do not let someone's status intimidate you or bamboozle you. They probably got to where they are today by being cruel to others. Read their character separately from their status or work.

Being in your emotional funk can distort your judgment, too. When you are emotionally down, you may be harsher to judge others in your state of bitterness. You may also be more vulnerable to kind actions from others.

Unfortunately, manipulators are great at spotting when you are upset and offering a kind action to gain favour with you. Do not let your emotional state make you vulnerable in judgment.

Emotional wounds can make it hard for you to trust people. This is especially true after you have been through a divorce or bad break-up. As a result, you might judge the gender that you are attracted to unfairly. You may instantly dislike all people of that gender. Do not be so quick to write off people that you do not know. Use your scars as lessons to read people who remind you of those that have hurt you in the past, but do not make the mistake of thinking that the entire gender is bad. Give individuals a chance. Try to read them, for who they are, not who your ex was.

Don't Just Base It Off of Behaviour

Many people make the mistake of trying to read people off of behaviour alone. But often behaviour offers an incomplete and inaccurate picture. You must consider someone's biases, mood, and even the context of the situation. Often, you cannot know all of this information, so do not even attempt to read someone based on behaviour alone.

Sometimes the behaviour is inaccurate because it is fake. Many people are great at creating a façade. They appear normal and upstanding while hiding their horrendous internal flaws. Think of most serial killers. Often, they go to work, keep nice houses, and look like totally normal people. The world is shocked when they are finally caught with a basement full of hacked-up bodies and torture devices. Sexual deviants who get caught watching child porn are often politicians and businessmen with great jobs and normal outside appearances. While these examples are extreme, many people are adept at hiding their bad personalities under totally normal behaviour. Therefore, you cannot base judgments on the outward behaviour of others, as this behaviour can be faked and misleading.

Create a Baseline

Try to gauge a baseline of someone's normal behaviour. Watch for unusual mannerisms that a person often displays. Quirks and habits that you frequently observe in someone over time form the person's baseline.

A baseline does not take long to form once you become more adept at reading people with practice. FBI profilers will usually gather this information within the first fifteen seconds of meeting a person.

From this baseline, you can tell when someone is behaving abnormally. When someone is behaving abnormally, you can determine that something is going on. Perhaps the person is lying or is upset about something.

It is difficult to start a baseline on someone if you do not have a chance to observe him over some time and you are not yet adept at reading people in just a few seconds. Therefore, it is a good idea to watch for really odd behaviour. Behaviour that stands out as unusual may be a quirk or it may be a sign of something more ominous, such as deception. You may want to ask other people who know the person well if this behaviour is normal for him. If you cannot do that, then you simply must rely on your gut. But do not rely too much on behaviour to form judgments about people.

You can start a baseline just by asking someone how they are doing today. Watch how the person reacts. From there, you can determine what his or her normal mannerisms are. The more you talk, the more you can gather about the person's baseline. Does his eye tic often? Does he often gesticulate with his hands? Does he stutter normally, or is he normally articulate? Also, gauge the speed with which he speaks in normal conversation and the tone and pitch of his voice.

You must establish a baseline to tell when someone is behaving inconsistently. In addition, a baseline lets you know how a person is in normal settings. If a person is typically nervous, you can decide if you want to be around someone who is frequently nervous and therefore probably insecure with social anxiety. If a person is typically rude and blunt, you can determine if you want to deal with that kind of behaviour in the future.

Infer Things from the Initial Reaction

Of course, strangers tend to be tense in their initial behaviour toward you because they do not know you well. But a person's initial reaction to you indicates a lot of information about how he feels about himself and how he feels about other people. This initial reaction shows the hang-ups he may have and the guard that he puts up to protect himself or the façade that he erects to charm people that he meets for the first time. As a result, this reaction says a lot about who he is as a person and the things that you may expect from him as you get to know him better.

If he is initially rude, for instance, he may thaw and become nicer toward you, but you know that at heart he has his guard up against new people. You can then wonder why he has his guard up. He is probably a sensitive and insecure person with a lot of emotional baggage – he feels that he has to act tough and careless to avoid getting hurt.

Particularly articulate and charming people usually have a lot to hide. They are great at being around people and hiding who they are. They have designed behaviour that is intended to hook people. Very charming behaviour is often indicative of manipulative and deceptive personalities.

An overly nervous person usually has social anxiety and is rife with insecurities. This person will probably get more comfortable with you over time. However, you may want to avoid trusting him too much. As a general rule, insecure people are not reliable and will act in ways that are not always appropriate. Insecure people tend to have trust issues and they will act out in ways that are hurtful because they believe that they are not good enough. You are not responsible for the insecurities of another person, so do not allow such a person to burden you with his problems and doubts.

A person who acts too calm is probably also a sufferer of social anxiety. However, he is adept at projecting calmness to hide how nervous he is. Become suspicious of people who are just "too chill."

Also, watch for people who only want to talk about themselves. People who are obsessed with themselves and do not even try to ask you questions about themselves are typically very selfish. This behaviour will not change with time.

Another behaviour that will not change with time is someone negative, even on your first meeting. People like this are very toxic and will simply try to drag you down.

A person who talks about others shamelessly when he first meets you is also probably a chronic gossip. It is not normal for someone to start gossiping when he first meets you.

Positivity and enthusiasm are great signs in a person that you have just met. However, if someone talks too much of a big game and brags overly much, you can assume that this person is trying to impress you or even make up for something that he feels that he is lacking. Mild positivity and enthusiasm are a great sign but being overly enthusiastic is not.

Confidence and assurance of oneself is a good sign in a stranger. A person who is willing to introduce himself to you, look you in the eye, and talk to you is usually secure in himself. He has developed good social skills and hence might be a more sensitive friend, lover, or work associate. While you want to be wary of people who are too smooth and charming, someone who acts normal yet confident is usually a good person to know.

Ask Pointed Questions

If you want to get to know someone, feel free to ask him questions about himself. He will probably volunteer a lot of the information that you want to know. You do not even have to ask him things to find out a lot of information about who he is as a person, what he likes, and what he is looking for from his association with you. This is why you should be a good listener.

But if he does not volunteer what you want to know, then ask. It is best to ask pointed questions and not be vague. If you are vague, you run the risk of miscommunication. As an adult, there is no use or time for games anymore. You know that you cannot be a mind reader, and neither can anyone else. So, ask what you want to know without shame.

You do not want to appear like you are interrogating someone. Asking rapid- fire questions can put a person off. Asking overly personal questions about someone's life, family, or personality is also off-putting. But do not be afraid to ask general, socially acceptable questions whenever there is a break in the conversation.

Monitor a person in how he answers your questions. Since you have already more or less established a good baseline, you can tell when there are inconsistencies in his responses. If his gestures, tone, pitch, or eye contact suddenly shifts away from his baseline, then you can tell that he is not being truthful or that a question makes him uncomfortable for some reason. You can change the subject or pursue it more, depending on your goal in communication with him.

Word Choice is Important

How a person talks indicate a lot about what he is feeling and thinking. Listen for keywords that indicate his intentions and his basic state of mind. The words that he chooses say a lot about how he is as a human being and what he is feeling at the moment. If you are meeting someone for the first time, remember that the initial meeting speaks volumes about who a person is inside. How he chooses to speak to you right off the bat indicates a lot about who he is generally.

Someone who uses very harsh, aggressive language is an aggressive person, or else he is currently in an angry mood. You never want someone to show you anger when you first meet – this indicates that the person may have an anger management problem.

Someone who uses very vague wording is possibly passive-aggressive and trying to skirt around a hard subject. This type of person is not able to be direct. Expect games and behaviour like shirking responsibility. If this person wrongs you, he will probably never admit to it and apologize. If he has a problem with you, he will probably never tell you to your face, but rather will hint about it or tell everyone else how he feels except for you.

Another troubling sign is when someone repeatedly says sorry or seems to take the blame for things. This type of person is very sinecure and blames him for everything.

Someone who uses conceited language, such as bragging about how he just won "another" award, indicates how proud he is of himself. Watch for people who brag too much about themselves. These people are usually narcissistic and egotistical or else they are overcompensating for feelings of inadequacy.

A person who uses very critical language is probably an overly judgmental person or a perfectionist. Watch for someone who nit-picks everything. This is a trait that will not lessen with time. If anything, it will only grow worse with time.

Most people use "I" terms more frequently than any other. This is not a troubling sign, but someone who uses more "we" terms is a better team player who is looking to collaborate with you. Someone who uses more ""your" terms are focused on you. This can be a great sign that someone is focused on pleasing you and getting to know you, or else it can be a worrisome sign that someone is trying to manipulate you. Watch for other word choices to tell the difference. If someone is asking you about what you like or who you are, then that is usually a sign that he wants to get to know you or find out how to best please you. This is a great sign on a date, a new friend, or a person that you are thinking about hiring for a service. But if he seems to be fishing for pertinent information with overly personal questions, if he keeps trying to find ways that he can commiserate with you so that you will confide in him, or if he is using fancy language and flattery to make you feel ingratiated and charmed by him, then that is a bad sign that he is trying to get an emotional hook into you to manipulate you.

A good sign that someone is being shifty is vague language. Someone who refuses to answer yes or no questions is probably lying. Someone who uses confusing language is probably deliberately creating a sort of mirage of vagueness to hide something.

READING PEOPLE THROUGH THEIR PHOTOGRAPHS

There are no escaping people's pictures in the age of a constantly buzzing social media feed. Like it or hate it, people are going to pictures of themselves. However, the good news from the perspective of a person analyzer is you can gather plenty of clues for speed-reading people even before you meet them simply by learning to read their photographs.

Imagine gaining some clues about a prospective employee before they come down for a face or face interview or learning more about a client before negotiating an important deal with them. How about picking the right date by gather insights about his or her personality through their social media images? Every image of a person holds a fascinating amount of information, meaning, and an indication of his or her emotional state. We only have to be perceptive enough to watch out for these clues. Sometimes, we are so overcome by the aesthetics of the image or the photography that we completely miss the emotions behind the image.

This chapter attempts to offer you some insights into how people's photographs can be used for interpreting their values, personality, and behavioural traits. There are some obvious and some subtle pointers about decoding an individual's personality through their photos. You will learn to find more meaning and context within the images rather than viewing them as random shots.

Do Not Rush

Since photographs capture moments where time freezes, you need to study the image carefully to avoid any biases or inaccurate readings about something that may have happened in a microsecond. This may be contrary to the fast-speed, short span of attention, limited energy, and multi-tasking disposition we display. Hit the brain's pause button, do some deep breathing and get yourself into slow motion before you begin analyzing people through their images. You need to approach the art of analyzing people with both curiosity and compassion.

Do not leave out any details Look at the entire image. What is it that holds your attention when you first look at the picture? What are the conspicuous aspects of the image? Slowly move your attention and awareness to the other parts of the images. Look at it from different angles and perspectives.

Pull the image closer to your vision to detect elements that would otherwise go unnoticed. There are plenty of subtle details that your eye may miss if you do not view them closely. Turning the image upside down or sideways allows you to view it from an unusual perspective, which can change your entire viewpoint about the image. You will end up noticing things you would not have otherwise noticed.

Subjective Reactions

What is it that strikes you the most about an image when you see it for the first time? What emotions, feelings, thoughts, and sensations overcome your mind when you look at the image on an instinctive level? Think of a single descriptive word or phrase as a caption or title for the image that captures your spontaneous reaction to the image.

Do you think the picture represents pride, anger, anxiety, relief, frustration? confinement, exhaustion, success, elation, exhilaration, smoothness, rage, sadness, and other compelling emotions? Your gut-level reaction offers a clue on what you are thinking about the person.

While observing or analyzing people through their photographs, one of the most important considerations is your instant or immediate reaction. However, you will need to go beyond the first impression. You will have to apply some amount of free association to analyze the person. Through free association, you are focusing on all elements of the image. Here are some questions you can ask yourself to facilitate greater free association to analyze people through images.

- What does the picture remind you of?
- What is the predominant emotion expressed by the person in the image?
- What memories, incidents, and experiences can you pull out from your state of awareness on looking at the image?

- How would you title the image?

However, when you are analyzing people through their pictures, beware of psychologists' terms of projection. Projection is an unconscious process through which our feelings, emotions, experiences, and memories distort our perception of other people we are analyzing. You may invariably end up projecting your feelings and experiences to them than trying to identify their personality. This is especially true for more ambiguous images. You do not know if you are rightly empathizing with people reading them correctly or simply recalling your own experiences.

Sometimes, our subjective reactions get in the way of reading people accurately. However, overcome this tricky situation and identifying when your own experiences and biases are getting in the way of analyzing people will help you be a more effective people analyzer.

Facial Expressions

Human beings are innately expressive when it comes to tuning in to other people's facial expressions. What is your first reaction to looking at the person's face in the photograph? Psychologists have recognized seven basic emotions in a person – surprise, contempt, fear, sadness, anger, disgust, and happiness. Keep these seven basic emotions in mind while analyzing people's expressions in images. At times, the expressions are underplayed or subtle, which makes it challenging to pin down the basic emotion.

Look for pictures where the person may not be aware that they are being clicked since that can be a more accurate representation of their subconscious mind.

Relationships

Again, you can tell a lot about the relationship between people by looking at their photographs. If a person is leaning in the direction of another person, there may be attraction or affection between the people. Similarly, if people are leaning in the opposite direction from each other, the relationship may lack warmth. If you notice a person clinging to their partner's arm in almost every photograph, he or she may most likely be insecure about losing their partner. It may reveal a deep sense of insecurity or fear of losing their partner.

Try to predict the relationship between people through their body language in images. This can also be done in any public place where you have some time at hand to check people's body language, relationship equations, and reactions. What are their feelings, emotions, thoughts, and attitudes towards each other? Is there a pattern in the manner through which people touch, lean towards each other or look at one another? Does their body language reveal a lack of connectedness?

One of my favorite pastimes when it comes to analyzing people is looking at the photographs of celebrity couples and trying to read the nature of their relationships and/or their personalities through their body language and expressions. I try to analyze if the image reveals intimacy, affection, and positivity? Or it demonstrates tension, disharmony, and conflict? Akeret, a well-known psychologist, believes that a photograph can also predict a relationships' future.

Some signs of comfort include smiling, holding hands, titling heads in the direction of their partner. Hip to hip posture may indicate things are going great between the couple. How is the palmer touch? If it is touching with the full hand, the partners are close and affectionate. On the other hand, fingertips or fist touching can be a sign of being distant and reserved. Crossing legs may mean that they weren't very comfortable or open at the time the picture was taken. If you find a person crossing their arms or legs in almost every photograph, they may be suspicious, doubtful, cynical, and unenthusiastic by nature.

Profile Pictures and Personality Traits

A big body of research suggests that human beings tend to assess one another's personality through a quick glimpse. This is exactly why first impressions are so lasting. It takes us only three to four seconds to form an impression about a person through their verbal and non-verbal clues. Sometimes, they may not even say anything, and we can subconsciously tune in to personality.

A recent research study reveals that you do not even have to meet a person once to form an opinion about him or her. All you need is a glance at their Facebook or even Tinder profile picture to gauge their personality. Here are the big five personality traits that are revealed through a person's profile picture.

The big five is pretty much the same to a scientific classification of personalities as Briggs-Myers is for recruitment. This personality approach classifies personalities based on five fundamental traits, namely introversion- extroversion, agreeableness, openness to new experiences, conscientiousness, and neuroticism.

A glance at your social media profile picture is sufficient for you to rate people correctly on the five fundamental dimensions. In research conducted by PsyBlog, it was observed through a scientific analysis of the profile pictures of thousands of social media participant personalities that there were very specific and consistent patterns when it came to each of the five personality attributes.

For example, people scoring high on conscientiousness used images that were natural, filter-free, bright, and vibrant. They were not afraid to express a large number of emotions through their pictures. They displayed a higher number of emotions through their images than all other personality types.

You will also find people scoring high on openness taking the most amazing shots. They are creative, innovative, and resourceful. They will play a lot with applications and filters owing to their creativity. Their pictures will be more artistic, unique, and feature greater contrasts. Generally, people who score high on openness have their faces occupy more space than any other feature in the photograph.

Extraversion folks will have perpetually broad smiles plastered on their faces. They will use collages and may surround their profile picture with used vibrant images. On the other hand, simple images with very little color or brightness are a strong indication of neuroticism. These pictures are likely to display a blank expression or in extreme cases may even conceal their face, according to the blog.

Agreeable people may often seem to the nicest people to get along with among all personality types. However, turns out, they aren't great photographers. Agreeable people are known to post unflattering images of themselves! However, even with the poor or unflattering images of themselves, they will be seen smiling or displaying a positive expression. The images will be vibrant, positive, and lively.

WHAT IS MANIPULATION?

Brainwashing and hypnosis are the two forms of mind control that are most known. While these two are important to understanding the function of mind control and how it all works, they are not the only available options. Others can be used – and are often more effective in the short term than either brainwashing or hypnosis. These particular tactics can be used in everyday situations. For example, it can be used in normal conversations a person may have with others.

The most important thing to remember about the forms of mind control is that they are more likely to occur in a person's daily life with the people they know and trust. A person will not put their subject into isolation or force them into an altered state of mind, as with brainwashing. Instead, they will employ different techniques to change the way their subject thinks. The three types of mind control that fit into this category include manipulation, persuasion, and deception. While manipulation may not put the person who is employing the tactic in harms' way or cause any immediate danger, it is set up to work in a deceptive and underhanded way to change the behaviour, viewpoint, and perception that the intended subject has in regards to a particular topic or situation.

What Is Manipulation?

This book will deliberate and discuss manipulation in terms of psychological manipulation. It is defined as a social influence working to alter individuals' behaviours or perceptions, or the subject, through deceptive, abusive, or underhanded methods. The manipulator works to advance his interests, usually to the detriment of another. Hence, most of their techniques are considered deceptive, abusive, exploitative, and devious. Whereas social influence is not completely negative – when a group or an individual is being manipulated, there is a likelihood of causing them harm. Social influence is regularly perceived to be harmless, such as a doctor persuading their patients to adopt healthy habits. This is true of any social influence that is not unduly coercive and can respect the right of those involved to choose. Alternatively, social influence can be destructive and looked down upon, especially if an individual tries to have his/her way and use people against their will.

Emotional or psychological manipulation is seen as a form of coercion and persuasion. For the most part, people will see this as abusive or deceptive. Those who decide to employ manipulation will attempt to control the behaviour of those around them. The manipulator will have some end goal in mind and will work through various forms of abuse to coerce those around them into helping the manipulator reach their final goal. Often emotional blackmail will also be involved.

Those who practice manipulation use brainwashing, mind control, or bullying strategies to get other people to finish their duties. The subject may not want to carry out the duties, but they may feel like they have no option because of the techniques used on them. Most manipulative people lack suitable caring and sensitivity towards other people – hence, they may not have an issue with their actions. Other Machiavellian may just want to attain their goal and would not be concerned with who has been hurt or bothered along the way. Along with that, manipulative individuals are often afraid to get into a healthy relationship because they fear others will not accept them. Someone who has a manipulative personality will often have the inability to be responsible for their problems, behaviours, and life. Because they are unable to accept responsibility for these issues, the manipulator will employ manipulation techniques to persuade someone else to do so.

Manipulators can often use the same tactics found in other forms of mind control to get the influence they want over others. One of the most commonly used tactics is known as emotional blackmail. This is where the manipulator will inspire guilt or sympathy in the individuals they try to manipulate. These two emotions are chosen since they are considered the two strongest of all human emotions – they are the most likely to drive others to act in the way the manipulator desires. The manipulator will then be capable of taking complete advantage of the victim, using the guilt or sympathy that he has created to force others into assisting them in meeting their targets. The manipulator may be capable of creating these emotions, but he can also inspire levels of guilt or sympathy that are out of proportion for the ongoing situation. For example, a manipulator can make a situation like missing a party seem like missing something very significant, like an interview.

Another tactic that has been successful for many manipulators is using a form of abuse commonly referred to as crazy-making. The tactic is frequently aimed at instilling self-doubt in the subject manipulated – typically, this self- doubt becomes so strong that some victims may begin to believe that they are going crazy. At times, the manipulator will use forms of passive-aggressive actions to cause crazy-making. They might also choose to show support or approval of the subject verbally, but then give non-verbal cues that show contradictory meanings. The manipulator often tries to undermine certain behaviours or events while showing his support for that same behaviour. Just in case the manipulator is found in the act, he will use denial, rationalization, justification, and the trickery of ill intent to escape the misfortune.

One of the biggest issues with psychological manipulators is that they are never able to find out what other people around them will need, and they may lose the capability to meet or even consider these needs. This does not excuse the behaviour they are doing. A manipulator will often fail to consider or prioritize the needs of others so that they can perform manipulative duties without feeling shame or guilt. This makes it difficult to stop the behaviour and rationally explain why the manipulator stops. Due to these behaviours, a manipulator may find it difficult to form meaningful and long-lasting friendships and relationships. This is because the people they are with will often feel used and will have difficulty trusting the manipulator. The problem with forming relationships goes both ways – the manipulator may fail to recognize other people's needs, while the other person may be unable to create the required emotional connections or confidence with the manipulator.

Requirements to Successfully Manipulate

A successful manipulator must have tactics at hand that will make them successful at using people to achieve their own final goal. While there are several theories on what makes a manipulator, we will look at the three requirements that have been set out by a successful psychology author known as George K. Simon. According to Simon, the manipulator will need to:

1. Be capable of determining their intended subject's vulnerabilities to determine the techniques that will be the most efficient in meeting their objectives.
2. Be capable of concealing their aggressive intentions and behaviours from the subject.
3. Have some ruthlessness levels readily available so that they do not have to deal with any uncertainties that may arise as a result of harming the victims if it reaches that point. This harm can be both emotional and physical.

The first requirement that a manipulator must accomplish to successfully manipulate his subjects is to conceal their aggressive intentions and behaviours. If the manipulator moves around being mean and telling every person his plans, then no individual is likely to stick around for long to undergo manipulation. Rather, he needs to be capable of concealing his thoughts from other people and behave as if everything is okay and normal. Often, those who are being manipulated will not realize it, at least not in the beginning. The manipulator will be sweet, act like their best friend, and maybe assist them in solving problems.

Next, the manipulator will need to find out what the vulnerabilities of their intended subjects are. This can help them establish the techniques that need to be used to reach their overall goal. At times the manipulator can do this step through a little bit of observation, while other times, they will need to interact with the subject before coming up with the full plan.

The third requirement is that the manipulator needs to be ruthless. It will no go well if the manipulator puts in all their effort only to be concerned about how the subject will feel in the end. If they did truly care about the subject, they would not be carrying out this plan. A manipulator should not care about the subject at all – he/she does not care if the subject suffers any harm, either physical or emotional, as long as the overall goal is met. One reason manipulators are so successful is because the subject often does not realize that he is being manipulated until later. He may think that everything is fine – he may think that perhaps he has gotten a new friend in the manipulator. The manipulator may use various techniques that may include emotional blackmail to get his way at the end.

HOW DARK PSYCHOLOGY WORKS

This chapter will explain one of the essential principles as you progress through future manuscripts broadening this construct. The following are the six principles that must be understood to achieve Dark Psychology ultimately.

1. Dark Psychology is a global part of the human condition. This aspect is maintained by all societies and the people who live in them. The most kind-hearted individuals have this realm of wickedness, but they never act on it – meaning that they have lower rates of violent ideas and sensations.

2. It is the study of the human condition as it relates to people's thoughts, feelings, and assumptions about their innate potential to prey on others for no apparent, definite reasons. Considering that all behaviour is purposive, goal-oriented, and conceptualized using modus operandi, Dark Psychology puts forth the idea that the closer an individual attracts the "black hole" of beautiful wickedness, the less likely he/she has a purpose in inspirations. It is presumed that beautiful evil is never gotten to because it is infinite – however, Dark Psychology thinks some have come close.

3. The background is loaded with instances of this unexposed propensity to disclose itself as active, harmful habits. Modern psychiatry and psychology define the psychotic as a predator lacking remorse for his activities. Dark Psychology says there is a continuum of intensity ranging from thoughts, as well as sensations, of physical violence to extreme victimization and physical abuse without a practical objective or inspiration.

4. In this continuity, the severity of the Dark Psychology is not made less or more severe by victimization actions, but rather stories out a variety of inhumanity. A straightforward comparison would be Ted Bundy versus Jeffrey Dahmer. Both were severe psychopaths who committed atrocities. The difference is Dahmer committed his godawful murders for his delusional demand for friendship while Ted Bundy murdered, and also sadistically brought upon discomfort out of great demented wickedness. Both would be greater on the Dark Continuum, yet one, Jeffrey Dahmer, can be better recognized using his psychotic hopeless requirement to be enjoyed.

5. Dark Psychology thinks all people have the potential for physical violence. This potential is innate in all people, and different interior, as well as external variables, raise the probability for this possibility to show up right into unstable habits. These habits are predatory, as well as at times – they can function without factor. Dark Psychology assumes the predator-prey vibrant becomes misshaped by human beings. Dark Psychology is entirely a human sensation and is shared by no other living being. Physical violence and even chaos may exist in various other living organisms, but humankind is the only variety that can do so without purpose.

6. An understanding of the underlying reasons and triggers of Dark Psychology would better allow the culture to recognize, identify, as well as reduce the dangers inherent in its influence. Discovering the ideas of Dark Psychology serves as a double beneficial feature. Initially, accepting most of us have this possibility for evil allows those with this expertise to reduce the probability of it erupting. And second, comprehending the tenets of Dark Psychology fits our original transformative objective for struggling to make it through.

The goal of this chapter is to enlighten others by increasing their self-awareness, developing a standard change of their truth for the better, and motivating those to tell others to embark on the path of discovery to reduce the possibility of succumbing to those had by the pressures explored by it. If you have been a victim or prey of the guided killer, do not feel humiliated since we all experience some kind of victimization at one time or another in our lives.

Most of us have a dark side. It becomes part of the human condition, but it is agreed that it is not well recognized. An undesirable reality is that Dark Psychology lurks on our outskirts patiently to strike. As previously stated, Dark Psychology encompasses all manner of terrible and violent habits. The mindless cruelty to animals is a prime example of this. Pet misuse is both ferocious and psychopathic. As recent studies have suggested, animal cruelty is associated with a higher probability of committing violence against humans.

On the milder end of the Dark Psychology spectrum is vandalism of other residential property or the increasing levels of violence in video games that children and teenagers advocate during the holiday season. Destruction and a child's desire to play terrible computer games are mildly contrasted to overt violence but are explicit examples of this global human attribute. The vast majority of humankind denies and hides its existence, yet still, the components of Dark Psychology silently hide underneath the surface in all people.

It is universal and almost everywhere throughout society. Some religious beliefs specify it as a real entity they call Satan. Some cultures rely on the presence of evil forces as being the wrongdoers causing malicious activities.

By examining the origin and nature of Dark Psychology, we can understand how a normal, well-socialized person can end up committing a mistake no one could have predicted. Since the beginning of recorded history, wrongs committed by one human against another have occurred at any time of day or night. Although horrifying, it is incredible how decent people can participate in or enable such atrocities to occur.

Thousands of these wrongdoings can be seen in the background. The holocaust during World War II, as well as ethnic cleansing currently taking place in neighbouring countries, are just a few examples. Cases abound with the residues of what Dark Psychology has caused. As explained above, Dark Psychology is alive and well and also requires a close examination. As you continue to discover the tenets and foundation of Dark Psychology, a cognitive structure of understanding will be established slowly.

Dark Continuum

The Dark Continuum is a crucial element to understanding the dark side of humankind. The Dark Continuum is a fictional conceptual line or concentric circles that all criminal, terrible, deviant, and vicious habits fall. The Dark Continuum includes thoughts, feelings, assumptions, and actions experienced or done by humans. The continuum varies from light to severe as well as from purposive to pointless.

Physical manifestations of Dark Psychology are more severe and located to the right of the Dark Continuum. Emotional symptoms of Dark Psychology lie to the left of the continuum. The Dark Continuum is not a scale of intensity, ranging from poor to worse, but it does specify types of victimization in the ideas and activities involved. Once the Dark Continuum thesis is expanded, you will undoubtedly have a theoretical illustrated line depicting all forms of Dark Psychology ranging from moderate and purposeful to extreme and purposeless.

Dark Variable

The Dark Element is defined as the realm, location, and also potential that exists in all of us – as it is inherent in the human condition. Because it is difficult to highlight using the created expression, this is one of the more abstract aspects of Dark Psychology. According to an online dictionary, a variable is anything that contributes causally to an outcome, such as a variety of elements figured out the issue. This section will undoubtedly make a significant attempt to theorize for you how Dark Aspect appears as an equation.

The Dark Aspect is not a mathematical formula, but a theoretical one. The Dark Element is a collection of occasions that a person experiences, which enhances their probability of participating in predacious habits. Although research study has suggested that youngsters who mature in violent homes become abusers themselves, this does not imply that all mistreated children grow up being violent transgressors. This is merely just one element of a wide range of experiences and scenarios that contribute to the Dark Variable.

The number of components that are involved in the Dark Factor equation is enormous. It is not the number of factors that cause Dark Element to become extreme. However, it is the impact that those experiences have on an individual's subjective processing that makes the Dark Aspect dangerous. Some of these aspects consist of genes, family member's characteristics, emotional knowledge, peer acceptance, personal handling, and developmental turning points, and also experiences.

Dark Singularity

The Dark Singularity is an academic principle comparable to the interpretation of singularity in the middle of a black hole. This illustrates the concept of the Dark Selfhood – astronomy, as well as cosmology is used as an allegory to define this principle. In astrophysics, the singularity is the outright centre of a black hole that is unbelievably tiny, yet thick in mass beyond mathematical comprehension. The theory recommends that the uniqueness is so dense and powerful, contemporary laws of physics and their mathematical equations come to be knotted.

A black hole is the massive expanse of room bordering the singularity – therefore, abundant light cannot leave its grip. At the center of all galaxies, the Milky Way is an all-powerful great void with a considerably small singularity at its facility chock packed with remarkable energy. The Dark Singularity, as it puts on Dark Psychology, is the absolute center of the Dark Psychology world. Simply put, the Dark Selfhood is constructed from immaculate evil & unadulterated pure malevolence. Likewise, part of the human condition is the Dark Singularity that no person ever reaches. The person who comes closest to this is the innovative and extreme psychotic who preys on others with minimal inspiration or objective for his activities.

Because all behaviour is purposeful, the Dark Selfhood is an ideal destination that was never reached. The Dark Selfhood is approaching but has not yet arrived. The core of Dark Selfhood is best described as "Predators That Victim Without Purpose". The closer a person approaches the Dark Selfhood, a lot more horrendous and sinister, their actions become. At the same time, their modus becomes much less deliberate.

When attempting to conceptualize Dark Singularity, a psychological and thoughtful principle to understand is that all behaviour is purposeful. Alfred Adler was a Millennium medical doctor as well as a psychotherapist that was a modern of Sigmund Freud, Carl Jung. He was an incredible philosopher who was honoured to have finished his postgraduate degree in the mid-1990s at the Adler College in Chicago, Illinois.

To now, this writer translates his world as defined by Alfred Adler, this fantastic clinical physician, and psychotherapist. Adler had several concepts of human habits, and these can be incorporated into the building of Dark Psychology. The three most valuable ideas from Adler for developing the concept are as follows.

MENTAL CONTROL

Another aspect in the field of dark psychology research is mental control. It can be a piece of both control and influence as the two strategies reach within your psyche and attempt to get you to accomplish something, think something, or tail another person's way for you. For some individuals, mental control can mean various things, such as control, influence, impact, and indoctrination. We will see mental control as an approach to change an individual's contemplations, convictions and control their activities.

Many people believe that brain control is one of the most all-around shrouded types of influence because the vast majority are not even aware that it is happening. It is also a reasonable procedure, which makes it more difficult for people to notice. Individuals under psyche control may believe they are deciding, but these decisions are made by someone else. You should know that the time it takes to control somebody's brain relies upon the used strategies: their character, individual elements, and social elements. Now and then, mental control can happen in light of physical power.

Mental control, like control and influence, is used in our daily lives. For the most part, we are unaware that the strategies used by publicizing organizations are a form of brain control. In any case, they are succeeding when they can persuade us that their product is the best. It does not imply that you must constantly be aware of what the promotion organizations are doing. The type of mental control you should be aware of is the dark kind. When it comes to mind control, you should be aware of the dangers it can pose. Focusing on promotions is a great way to practice how to monitor against mental control and figure out what procedures are being used.

Ways You Can Control People or Be Controlled

Individuals who need to control their brains can utilize any of the accompanying methods or systems that fall under control or influence. One of the most significant variables to recollect is that individuals who control others are incredible at understanding others. They can ordinarily determine what sort of individual they are managing before long. It encourages them to recognize what kind of system they can utilize and which one they cannot. It also enables them to comprehend what kind of individual you are. They need to know if you are enthusiastic and mentally strong, as this can make their job more difficult. They want to know if you are self-assured or affected.

Conduct Molding and Conditioning

Conduct molding, otherwise called alteration, is the way to get individuals to do what you need. You do this through a progression of remunerations and disciplines. It is used in child-rearing classes and brain research courses in school. You have to understand that behaviour adjustment is the demonstration of changing somebody's conduct. When the individual reliably follows the behaviour, they were instructed, it is known as social molding. A social alteration will consistently precede conduct molding.

Individuals who need to take responsibility for their minds exceed expectations in terms of behaviour change. This is because they must change your behaviour to condition you, which is the point at which they have complete control. They must ensure that the opposition towards the changing practices is minimal, or else they will wind up battling molding. You may then get on to their brain control inclinations and do what you can to end it.

Conviction Change Processes

Perhaps the most important key to changing somebody's perspective is to focus on changing their conviction forms. This implies that you do more than just change their conviction – you also change their thinking.

Brain research is probably the most important subject in which mental controllers are competent. To deal with their points of view, a brain controller will consider how their objective thinks. This allows them to gain control of their target's brain. As a result, specialists are most likely the best model for mental control. In any case, advisors are attempting to help their clients change their behaviours to improve their lives. Mental controllers must change the rules of their objectives so that they can gain control of the individual.

Undercover Belief Changes

You do not have to use pictures to persuade someone to change their convictions. Most brain controllers that are attempting to control you to gain the upper hand will not focus on images. This is because you will get on too effectively, especially at first. This does not mean they will never place- specific images in your mind – It simply means that they will focus more on covert conviction changes.

Psyche controllers should ensure that they have your trust, regard, and association with them. Without these variables, they would not have the option to significantly change your convictions. They are additionally talented at tying down. This is because they recognize that feelings are frequently a reliable guide for individuals and do not know how to control their emotions. Mental controllers who can maintain their emotions well will struggle to be effective with this technique.

The initial step for the psyche controller will lead you to the behaviour they need to change. At the point when they do this, they will attempt to be inconspicuous in their endeavours. They would not act like they need to change your behaviour straightforwardly. Nonetheless, they could refer to how it affected them as this will evoke an enthusiastic reaction from you.

When you give them a feeling, they will pull out the mooring method. Whatever behaviour they want you to change, they will quietly tell you what you should do. While this will most likely take some time, you will notice a change in your behaviour. Every time you do something that your life partner feels is not right, you will remember how you felt when you talked about it. After a while, you will gradually stop engaging in this behaviour because it gives you a negative inclination.

Rewards and Consequences

It is now difficult for adults to maintain control because they are rewarded and punished for their actions. This happens a few times a day, but we only notice it once in a while. For example, if you complete a task, your manager will compliment you. This will have a negative effect, making you more conscious of your time on the board. You will be bound to make cut-off times later on.

Mental controllers will also adhere to the prize and outcome framework. If you go out with your friends after your loved one has revealed something to you, they will give you the silent treatment for two or three days. This will make you realize that they are perplexed by you, which will make you lose faith in yourself. While you may not understand why they are doing this because you just went out with a few friends, your emotions will control you more than your thoughts. When your better half tells you that they would prefer you to stay at home rather than go out, you are bound to think about staying at home. This does not imply that you will.

The I to You Shift

This is basic in the usual discussion, which implies it very well, though it may not be obvious. Individuals who are attempting to control their brain, on the other hand, will frequently project their story onto you. This implies that instead of saying "I," they will say "you."

There are a few explanations behind this. One reason is that it gives both of you a sense of belonging. This is something that academics frequently use to positively interact with their audience. In any case, when it comes to mind control, this is used in a progressively negative manner. When examining a negative story that can cast you in a negative light, psyche controllers who need to work on your self-assurance will use the word "you". Even if you are aware that you did not do this and that you are not a part of the story, it enters your psyche and can cause you to accept that you have accomplished something comparable in your life. As a result, your feelings toward the character in the story are the same as your feelings toward yourself.

They Will Think for You

Individuals who need to intellectually control you will have no trouble starting to think for you. Their trick is that they will frequently begin to settle on a choice for you where it truly does not matter. You could be inspecting something and informing them, "I'm not sure what I think. Let me think about it." This is an open way for somebody who needs to control your brain. This discloses to them that you need assistance settling on a choice. Subsequently, if they step in to decide on the choice for you unobtrusively, it will not trouble you.

They will tell you something like, "I realize you are worried about everything else, so why not let me settle on the choice, and we will discuss it." Then, to appear as though they set aside an effort to settle on the choice, they will come to you somewhat later with their answer. They will act like you have a decision or act as they care about your opinion of their choice. Be that as it may, you genuinely do not have a decision. They are merely attempting to get you to believe that they can settle on choices for you.

They will, at that point, begin settling on more choices for you, without your authorization. However, you would not give much thought to these alternatives because they aren't particularly significant. They will stop getting information about anything at that point. Although they begin to limit your options, you will most likely not notice because you have grown accustomed to them thinking for you.

BRAINWASHING TO STOP BEING MANIPULATED

Brainwashing tends to be a little more "personal" and subtle. It often requires the victim to be isolated, and it is dependent on the individual or group of individuals who are brainwashing them. This is a favourite tactic of cults, religious groups, and yes, even your favourite sports teams.

Let us focus on national, televised sports, the most seemingly innocent form of cult worship. Billions of people all over the world tune in to watch football, baseball, swimming, car racing, cricket, volleyball, curling... the list goes on. Those same billions spend even more billions of dollars on tickets and travel to live games, merchandise, and the access to watch their favourite teams on their favourite channel in the comfort of their own home. What would happen if the Super Bowl didn't air in February? An honest, logical guess might be: "The world would end as we know it." Championship games of all kinds draw larger audiences than political rallies, religious observations, and even the release of the latest iPhone.

But let us wait and see what happens: Does it matter whether the Patriots win or lose the Super Bowl again? No, but every February, millions of television screens turn to the game, regardless of team affiliation. What kind of power is this?

A dangerous one, that's it. In the same way that a politician or businessman has a broad reach to emotionally manipulate an audience, large groups of brainwashers can reduce your consciousness to its bare essentials. Then it replaces that person's "personhood" with a false identity, a set of ideals, beliefs, likes, and dislikes.

How is the NFL or NHL capable of advertising and affiliations? The NFL is one of the largest and most prominent sponsors and advertisers of the United States military. Commercials for different branches play during breaks, certain games, and national anthems are dedicated to veterans, POWs, or current individuals serving. Players even don camouflage, military-inspired gear as part of this relationship.

Then there was the debate over the national anthem when Colin Kaepernick knelt in solidarity for all of his fellow people of colour brutalized by police violence. The NFL immediately launched a vociferous media campaign that was picked up by NFL fans everywhere. Soon, stickers, hats, and t-shirts could be found everywhere saying "I stand for the anthem".

The NFL took this opportunity to use their fan base's interests, as well as the hold they already had on loyal fans. As television ratings were dropping, the NFL created a problem that didn't exist and turned it into a media tornado – this unleashed their rhetoric on millions of viewers nationwide. It had a discernible effect by creating a reason for people to watch other than for the game itself.

The Fundamentals of Brainwashing

Many people tend to get hypnosis, CEM, NLP, and brainwashing confused. But brainwashing is not just a dark psychological technique. It is one identified by psychologists all over the world as well. It is not only a tool for sports teams, but it has also been the preferred method of recruiting members for cults for decades, if not centuries.

Brainwashing from here on out means the process of forcing an individual into accepting belief systems completely and utterly different than their own, often under pressure.

Cults are the simplest example of brainwashing because they are small groups of people who practice a form of religion or belief that appears sketchy, questionable, and possibly evil from the outside. Some examples of famous cults and their leaders include:

Jim Jones

Jim Jones is the leader of the People's Temple Cult. Jones was a zealous religious leader who convinced hundreds of his followers to participate in a mass murder/suicide by drinking poisoned Kool-Aid.

Children of God / Family International

This cult was founded by David "Moses" Berg in California in 1968. The members of this cult were encouraged to have sex with children to achieve "divinity". This cult still exists today on multiple continents and over 70 countries. This cult, in particular, was perpetuated by founder David Berg's master of propaganda writing and publishing, which drew new members to his group and kept older members close by.

Branch Davidians

This was a splintered extremist group of Seventh Day Adventists that had been in existence since the 1950s. It wasn't until leader David Koresh took over as leader that he began to claim that he was the Messiah and claimed all women and female children for his own. The group did believe that the end of the world was nigh, but many never got to see it. The cult was disbanded in1993 after a standoff with FBI agents that resulted in more than 80 deaths.

Realism

Followers of this cult, founded in 1974, believe that all life on Earth is scientifically created, thus, not organic, and challenging all prevalent scientific theories of evolution. The Raël creator is named Elohim, and that leaders within the movement are former aliens that will teach the earth how to carry on Raël traditions, including peace and mindfulness

What Makes Up a Cult

Now that we have a few examples of cults, let us dissect what makes up a cult. Usually, this small, strange group will have one or two leaders with strong personalities that lead their followers and often make decisions on their behalf.

Cults also usually seem very accepting at first, but that's because they are looking to increase their numbers. Do not mistake friendliness for desperation on their part.

Cults also make followers feel safe. The boisterous and charming leader is also a comforter – those who end up lost or confused by traditional religion are comforted and brought into the fold. Existential questions like "Why am I here?" and "What is my purpose in life?" are easily answered by the cult's lore (usually a cult will have a few strong oral storytellers, too).

Acceptance. Purpose. Belonging. The things people crave most of all are the things cults are most willing to dish out.

Cults and Brainwashing

Cults and brainwashing go together like peanut butter and jelly. The latter enables the former. In this book and this context, brainwashing is a type of total "reboot" of thought and framing of the mind. Again, unless the victim is perceptive, this technique will likely go unnoticed.

Before we return to cults, it is important to establish that this is not the only way brainwashing is used. For example, a dress code at your job could be brainwashing if you work there long enough for the brainwashing to work its way in.

EMOTIONAL INTELLIGENCE

Emotional Understanding can be defined as the ability to recognize, understand, and cope with our feelings as we perceive, understand, and influence others. This is being awake in the sense that our emotions can decisively and contrastively influence our behaviour. It also entails learning how to deal with these feelings, both our own and those of others, especially when under stress.

- When Might You Have to Deal with Your Emotional Intelligence?
- Dealing with testing connections Dealing with change
- Not having enough assets Giving and accepting input
- Dealing with mishaps and disappointment
- Meeting tight due dates
- Emotional Intelligence is worth twice as much as IQ and specialized abilities combined in determining the identity of the will.

Reasons For Improving Emotional Intelligence

Give the best you have to offer. Discover why your best self creates the best decisions.

- It allows for remarkable leadership. Individuals are administrators, not occupations. Outstanding pioneers bring out the best in their kin.
- Emotional intelligence promotes mindfulness. Understand the effect you have on the general population around you.
- It supports extraordinary workplace culture. Positive attitudes are infectious. Improve relationship quality and create a culture of responsibility.
- It achieves neuroscience-based change. Drive genuine conduct change with a program established in neuroscience and research.

Emotions go before the idea. At a point when feelings run high, they change how our minds work, lessening our intellectual capacities, basic leadership controls, and even relational aptitudes.

There is no approved psychometric test or scale for emotional intelligence, as there is for general intelligence. Many argue that emotional intelligence is not a genuine development, but a method for depicting relational abilities that pass by different names.

Notwithstanding this analysis, emotional intelligence intrigues the general public, just as in specific areas. A few businesses have fused emotional intelligence tests into their application or meeting forms, on the hypothesis that somebody with high emotional intelligence would make a superior employee or colleague.

While a few investigations have discovered a connection between emotional intelligence and employment execution – others have demonstrated no relationship and the absence of an experimentally substantial scale makes it hard to quantify or foresee somebody's emotional intelligence at work.

An emotionally insightful individual is both profoundly aware of his or her very own emotional states – cynicism, disappointment, misery, or something increasingly unpretentious – and ready to distinguish and oversee them. These individuals are, likewise, particularly sensitive to the feelings of others and their experiences. Luckily, these abilities can be sharpened.

Even though there are numerous sorts of intelligence, and they are often associated with each other – there are some extremely noteworthy contrasts between them.

Comparison between Social and Emotional Intelligence

Social intelligence is identified more with emotional intelligence than IQ because the two of them have to do with exploring social or emotional circumstances. These are two particular sorts of intelligence.

Emotional intelligence is increasingly identified with the present because it recognizes and oversees feelings at the time. In contrast, social intelligence employs a similar set of abilities and capacities, but it is frequently focused on the future. It enables you to comprehend your own emotions, personalities, and practices, as well as those of others, to achieve positive outcomes.

Psychology and Emotional Intelligence

Analysts have discovered that emotional intelligence improves one's understanding of intelligence. This consistently demonstrates that IQ is not everything, but the hypotheses on what, precisely, the other significant segments were varied enormously, and analysts could not agree on a single idea or thought.

When emotional intelligence was presented initially, clinicians acknowledged that it was the missing part of intelligence that they were studying.

EQ vs. Level of intelligence

EQ is emotional intelligence and is tied with recognizing feelings in ourselves, as well as other people, identifying with others, and conveying our sentiments.

The level of intelligence, on the other hand, is subjective intelligence because people understand it as the type that is frequently alluded to when the term "intelligence" is used.

Comprehending the course of events for the presentation and grasp of emotional intelligence inside brain research, we can begin with the work of Peter Salovey.

Peter Salovey's Research

In 1990, John Mayer and Peter Salovey aptly introduced emotional intelligence. According to them, it is the capacity to perceive, comprehend, use, and manage feelings adequately in regular, day-to-day existence. Their research sparked a surge of interest in emotional intelligence from scholarly sources and other forms of research.

The Research by Daniel Goleman

Following Mayer and Salovey's research, Goleman acquainted emotional intelligence with the rest of the world – different scientists and therapists started running with it. Daniel Goleman was an example of this kind of therapist. In 1995, he distributed his work that clarified everything.

Goleman believed that emotions were an important factor in development, especially for children. He proposed that promoting emotional and social learning in children to support their emotional intelligence would do more than just improve their learning abilities. It would help them succeed in school by reducing or eliminating the most distracting and destructive behaviour issues.

His proposition has been invited by the scientific community, and it is presently nearly underestimated that emotional intelligence may be similarly as significant – If not progressively significant – to singular accomplishment as IQ.

Travis Bradberry's Research

Following the research by Goleman, writers Travis Bradberry and Jean Greaves gained recognition by developing an interest in emotional intelligence and disseminating their research that lays out a well-organized plan for improving it. Greaves and Bradberry proposed nearly seventy proof- supported techniques for developing emotional intelligence by demonstrating mindfulness, self-administration, and mindfulness.

The writers guarantee that the research will allow you to understand your feelings, as well as other people's feelings. It also offers a test to demonstrate it.

Emotional Intelligence Framework

The numbers five and four significantly help in understanding what emotional intelligence is all about. There are five parts of the emotional intelligence model and four measurements to EQ.

The Five Aspects of the EQ Model

As indicated by Daniel Goleman, the components of emotional intelligence are the following:

1.   Motivation
2.   Social Skills
3.   Self-Awareness
4.   Empathy
5.   Self-Regulation

Individuals with high EQs have progressively inborn inspiration. Individuals with high emotional intelligence are motivated within themselves to achieve their goals.

At long last, social aptitudes represent the final piece of the emotional intelligence puzzle. These abilities are what enable individuals to communicate socially with one another and effectively explore social situations. Individuals with high emotional intelligence have great social skills and can pursue their goals and achieve the results they require when interacting with others.

Mindfulness is characterized as the capacity to perceive and comprehend personal feelings. It is the beginning of emotional intelligence as managing our understandings – having sympathy for other people depends on distinguishing and perceiving feelings within our persona.

Empathy is characterized as the capacity to comprehend the feelings of others and perceive how you feel that you are in their shoes. It is not about identifying with, approving, or acknowledging conduct – only that you can wear their shoes and understand what is happening to them.

If it is important to let the people around you know that you care for them and are willing to be there for them in times of need. The advantage is that in your time of need, you will be able to get help from the same people, who will help you through your difficulties.

Self-guidance is above and beyond. We should not only be able to perceive our feelings if we want to have a high EQ. However, we should also be able to express, direct, and supervise them appropriately.

The Four Dimensions of Emotional Intelligence

According to EQ's "founding fathers," Mayer and Salovey, the components of EQ that structure the order of emotional aptitudes and capacities are as follows:

1. Utilizing feelings to encourage thought.
2. Recognizing feelings.
3. Overseeing feelings.
4. Understanding feelings.

The principal measurement, which is recognizing the feeling, identifies with monitoring and perceiving other individuals' physical and mental states, such as experiencing physical torment or experiencing fatigue, recognizing feelings of other individuals, communicating personal feelings and requirements precisely and fittingly, and recognizing exact, fair emotions and incorrect, deceptive sentiments.

Using feelings to encourage thought entails diverting and organizing your speculation based on the emotions associated with those musings, producing feelings that will encourage better judgment and memory, profiting from mindset changes so you can value different perspectives, and utilizing emotional well-being to improve critical thinking abilities and imagination.

The component of comprehending feelings incorporates perceiving the connections among different feelings, seeing the reasons and results of feelings, perceiving multifarious sentiments and conflicting positions, and comprehending the advances with feelings.

The last measurement, overseeing feelings, alludes to being available to both wonderful and disagreeable sentiments – observing and thinking about your feelings, drawing in, delaying, or isolating from an emotional state, and dealing with the feelings, both inside yourself and in others.

A state is a brief idea design, feeling, or conduct that is incidental and exceptionally reliant on the earth, just as a person's character. A trait can be described as a perpetual idea that is steady, durable, and moderately stable – with attributes that are substantially subject to character over the condition.

For what reason would it be advisable for us to think about building up our emotional intelligence aptitudes?

Having the ability to comprehend personal feelings is critical to perceiving what will enable you to thrive to advance. This is because we will be exceptionally socially adept as individuals.

Being emotionally aware will allow you to interact with others, improve your work presentation, strengthen your relationships, and much more.

Positivity and Emotional Intelligence

If you work in positive brain research in any capacity, for example, as a mentor, advisor, advocate, or teacher, you are probably aware of the benefits of increased emotional intelligence. Having the ability to perceive and successfully manage both good and bad feelings will help science professionals in their interactions with customers, improving both their exhibition and the prosperity rate of their customers.

Those who fail to use emotional intelligence will find that their mediations are ineffective. If your customers have trouble 'understanding' you, they will find it difficult to develop their emotional intelligence and be in a position of strength.

Success in Relationships

Controlling your emotions and understanding those around you are essential abilities to possess in everyday life. They not only help us live more joyful and beneficial lives, but they also help us get through difficult times to be successful.

Self-administration is the initial step, as we should figure out how to oversee ourselves before we can oversee sound, suitable associations with other people. Comprehending self-administration enables you to have control over yourself, to a limited degree, and ensure success in all circumstances.

Focusing on improving your relationships allows you to create solid connections and impart successfully in all situations, including opening up to others, expressing what is on your mind, influencing others, and being honest without affecting others.

BEHAVIOURAL TRAITS OF FAVORITE VICTIMS OF MANIPULATORS

There are certain characteristics and behavioural traits that make people more vulnerable to manipulation – and people with dark psychological traits know this full well. They tend to seek out victims who have those specific behavioural traits because they are essentially easy targets. Let us discuss six of the traits of the favourite victims of manipulators.

Emotional Insecurity and Fragility

Manipulators like to target victims who are emotionally insecure or emotionally fragile. Unfortunately for these victims, such traits are very easy to identify even in total strangers, so it is easy for experienced manipulators to find them.

Emotionally insecure people tend to be very defensive when they are attacked or when they are under pressure. This makes them easy to spot in social situations. A manipulator can tell how insecure a person is with a high degree of accuracy after only a few interactions. They will try to provoke their potential targets subtly, and then wait to see how the targets react. If the victim is overly defensive, manipulators will take it as a sign of insecurity, and they will intensify their manipulative attacks.

Manipulators can also tell that a target is emotionally insecure if he/she redirects accusations or negative comments. They will find a way to put you on the spot, and if you try to throw it back at them or to make excuses instead of confronting the situation head-on, the manipulator could conclude that you are insecure and therefore an easy target.

People who have social anxiety also tend to have emotional insecurity, and manipulators are aware of this fact. In social gatherings, they can easily spot individuals who have social anxiety. They then go after them to manipulate them. "Pickup artists" can identify the girls who seem uneasy in social situations by the way they present themselves. Social anxiety is difficult to conceal, especially to manipulators who are experienced at preying on emotional vulnerability.

Emotional fragility is different from emotional insecurity. Emotionally insecure people tend to show it all the time, while emotionally fragile people appear to be normal – but they break down emotionally at the slightest provocation. Manipulators like targeting emotionally fragile people because it is very easy to elicit a reaction from them. Once a manipulator finds out that you are emotionally fragile, he/she is going to jump at the chance to manipulate you because he/she knows that it would be fairly easy.

People with these characteristics are frequently targeted by opportunistic manipulators since emotional fragility is temporary. A person may be emotionally stable most of the time, but when they are going through a breakup, grieving, or dealing with an emotionally exhausting circumstance, they may feel emotional fragility. The more diabolical manipulators can earn your trust, bid their time, and wait for you to be emotionally fragile. Alternatively, they can use underhanded methods to induce emotional fragility in a person they are targeting.

Sensitive People

Highly sensitive people are those individuals who process information at a deeper level and are more aware of the subtleties in social dynamics. They have lots of positive attributes because they tend to be very considerate of others, and they watch their step to avoid causing people any harm, whether directly or indirectly. Such people tend to dislike any form of violence or cruelty, and they are easily upset by news reports about disastrous occurrences, or even depictions of gory scenes in movies.

Sensitive people also tend to get emotionally exhausted from taking in other people's feelings. When they walk into a room, they have the immediate ability to detect other people's moods, because they are naturally skilled at identifying and interpreting other people's body language cues, facial expressions, and tonal variations.

Manipulators like to target sensitive people because they are easy to manipulate. If you are sensitive to certain things, manipulators can use them against you. They will feign certain emotions to draw sensitive people in so that they can exploit them.

Sensitive people also tend to scare easily. They have a heightened "startle reflex," which means that they are more likely to show clear signs of fear or nervousness in potentially threatening situations. For example, sensitive people are more likely to jump up when someone sneaks up on them, even before they determine whether they are in any real danger. If you are a sensitive person, this trait can be very difficult to hide, and malicious people will be able to see it from a mile away.

Sensitive people also tend to be withdrawn. They are mostly introverts, and they like to keep to themselves because social stimulation can be emotionally draining for them. Manipulators who are looking to control others are more likely to target people who are introverted because that trait makes it easy to isolate potential victims.

Manipulators can also identify sensitive people by listening to how they talk. Sensitive people tend to be very proper – they never use vulgar language, and they tend to be very politically correct because they are trying to avoid offending anyone. They also tend to be polite, and they say please and thank you more often than others. Manipulators go after such people because they know that they are too polite to dismiss them right away – sensitive people will indulge anyone because they do not want to be rude, and that gives malicious people away.

Emphatic People

Emphatic people are generally similar to highly sensitive people, except that they are more attuned to the feelings of others and the energy of the world around them. They tend to internalize other people's suffering to the point that it becomes their own. In fact, for some of them, it can be difficult to distinguish someone's discomfort from their own. Emphatic people make the best partners because they feel everything you feel. However, this makes them particularly easy to manipulate, which is why malicious people like to target them.

Malicious people can feign certain emotions, and convey those emotions to emphatic people, who will feel them as though they were real. That opens them up for exploitation. Emphatic people are the favorite targets of psychopathic conmen because they feel so deeply for others. A conman can make up stories about financial difficulties and swindle lots of money from emphatic people.

The problem with being emphatic is that because you have such strong emotions, you easily dismiss your doubts about people because you would much rather offer help to a person who turns out to be a liar than deny help to a person who turns out to be telling the truth.

Emphatic people have a big-hearts, and they tend to be extremely generous, often to their detriment. They are highly charitable, and they feel guilty when others around them suffer – even if it is not their fault and they cannot do anything about it. Malicious people have a very easy time taking such people on guilt trips. They are the kind of people who would willingly fork over their life savings to help their friends get out of debt, even if it means they would be ruined financially.

Malicious people like to get into relationships with emphatic people because they are easy to take advantage of. Emphatic people try to avoid getting into intimate relationships in the first place because they know that it is easy for them to get engulfed in such relationships and to lose their identities in the process. However, manipulators will doggedly pursue them because they know that once they get it, they can guilt the emphatic person into doing anything they want.

Fear Of Loneliness

Many people are afraid of being alone, but this fear is more heightened in a small percentage of the population. This type of fear can paralyze persons who feel it, leaving them vulnerable to abuse by malicious individuals. For example, many people stay in dysfunctional relationships because they are afraid – they are afraid that they will never find someone else to love them if they break up with an abusive partner. Manipulators can identify this fear in a victim, and they will often do everything they can to fuel it further to make sure that the person is crippled by it. People who are afraid of being alone can tolerate or even rationalize any kind of abuse.

The fear of being alone can be easy to spot in a potential victim. People with this kind of fear tend to exude some level of desperation at the beginning of relationships, and they can sometimes come across as clingy. While ordinary people may think of being clingy as a red flag, manipulative people will see it as an opportunity to exploit somebody. If you are attached to them, they can use manipulative techniques to make you even more dependent on them. They can withhold love and affection (e.g., by using the silent treatment) to make the victim fear that he/she is about to get dumped so that they act out of desperation and cede more control to the manipulator.

The fear of being alone is, for the most part, a social construct, and it disproportionately affects women more than men. For generations, our society has taught women that their goal in life is to get married and have children, so, even the more progressive women who reject this social construct are still plagued by social pressures to adhere to those old standards. That being said, the fact is that men also tend to be afraid of being alone.

People with abandonment issues stemming from childhood tend to experience the fear of loneliness to a higher degree. There are also those people who may not necessarily fear loneliness in general, but they are afraid of being separated from the important people in their lives. For example, lots of people end up staying in abusive or dysfunctional relationships because they are afraid of being separated from their children.

Fear Of Disappointing Others

We all feel a certain sense of obligation towards the people in our lives, but some people are extremely afraid of disappointing others. This kind of fear is similar to the fear of embarrassment and the fear of rejection because it means that the person puts a lot of stock into how others perceive him or her.

The fear of disappointing others can occur naturally, and it can be useful in some situations – parents who are afraid of disappointing their families will work to provide for them, and children who are afraid of disappointing their parents will study harder at school. In this case, the fear is constructive. However, it becomes unhealthy when it is directed at the wrong people, or when it forces you to compromise your comfort and happiness.

When manipulators find out that you have a fear of disappointing others, they will try to put you in a position where you feel like you owe them something. They will do certain favors for you, and then they will manipulate you into believing that you have a sense of obligation towards them. They will then guilt you into complying with any request whenever they want something from you.

HOW THE DARK TRIAD CAN BE APPLIED

We must understand the three parts of the Triad and the different ways that it can manifest itself in actual behaviour. Let us look at the behaviours that can show this in each of the three Triad areas.

Machiavellian Actions

They are almost as concerned with it as they are with pursuing their self-interest above everything else. So, how do you expect a Machiavellian person to act? This action can be hard to recognize because these kinds of people are, in their nature, adept at being able to hide all their true intentions from public scrutiny. However, there are a few different signals that you can see when you are dealing with a Machiavellian person.

First off, these people are going to have a very clear distinction between what they are and how they come across when they are out in public. For example, there are a lot of cases where a serial murderer was able to get away with the crimes for a very long time – and the main reason for this is because their outward image is so far removed from what people imagine a murderer to be like.

An excellent example of this could be a religious leader. This person would spend time running their congregation, doing charity work, and seem like they always help regular people. But then on the side, they will commit horrific acts of violence. This person's public actions are the masks that hide the private side away from scrutiny for a very long time.

Of course, there are examples of this distinction in areas that aren't as extreme as serial murder. There are many talks where the leaders in the field of business were able to ruthlessly cut jobs to get profits, without worrying about the people it would hurt. And these bosses, if they are talented with the work, can act like they are behaving in this manner because it is a necessity – rather than just because they want more money.

Another hallmark that you will run into with Machiavellianism is a willingness to exploit other people. Let us keep with the idea of someone who started working in a new office. Someone who is not a Machiavellian would look around that office and see that there is a room of different co-workers that they could get to know. But a newcomer, who is a Machiavellian, would see each person in front of them as another resource to exploit or use. Instead of seeing these people as fellow human beings, the Machiavellian individual would focus on finding weaknesses and other things to exploit when it works for them.

Another principle of Machiavellianism that comes from "The Prince" is the idea that the person will only keep their promise or their word when doing so will serve their self-interest. Many people believe that a Machiavellian person is not trustworthy, but this is not quite right. If it is going to serve their interests to keep their word, such as when they want to build up trust with their victim, they will keep their word. And in many cases, when this type of person is not able to keep their word, they will be able to do it in a way that can make them appear noble and even praiseworthy in the process – leaving them in a good light, even when they decide not to keep with the promise.

And the final hallmark that shows up for this kind of person is the ability to instill fear in others around them. This idea comes directly from "The Prince" which urges a person to be both loved and feared at the same time. If the person cannot be both, then the book states that it is better to be feared than loved. This concept regarding the desirability of being feared and loved at the same time is directly related to the trait of splitting up the private and the public perception. The perfect Machiavellian can then inspire obedience and fear in the people who are most likely to claim that they feel love stronger than fear as a result.

Psychopathic Actions

A psychopathic person's charm is a fairly common outward behaviour. It is more of a superficial charm and never a deep or genuine one. If you think about someone who is genuinely charming, you would be able to pinpoint that they have a very positive personality under the display of the behaviour. This is not something that you are going to see when a psychopath is trying to be charming.

Psychopaths can show all the signs of charm, including an interest in those around them, an apparent warmth, and physical attractiveness. But the inward motivation to these displays can be a red flag. Psychopaths are only using charm to achieve their goals. They recognize that presenting charm to someone will make them feel good, which the manipulator may take advantage of. Remember that charm is going to be calculated and shallow, just like everything else a psychopath does. There is not going to be any depth of feeling behind the behaviour.

Another sign of a psychopath is lying. Of course, lying is not enough to place someone in a psychopath's category, but when it is combined with other signs, it can be a problem. A psychopath will find that lying is very natural and can do it in a very convincing manner. They also would not show any signs of lying simply because they do not have an emotional attachment or any feelings of excitement, guilt, or shame about their lies. In a psychopath's mind, lying is just "doing what is needed at the time," nothing more and nothing less.

A lack of remorse is another feature that is going to show up with a psychopath. Many people who have committed crimes, such as murder, would show a sense of shame or guilt over what they do. But a psychopath is not able to feel remorse at all. They can do these actions and these crimes without any feelings about it. Linked to this is a lack of guilt. Most humans are going to feel at least a little guilty when they go against a moral norm.

But psychopaths are not going to think in terms of what is right and what is wrong. They look at things in terms of what is useful and what is not useful to them. Remorse and guilt do not fit into this at all.

Psychopaths are often incapable of empathy. They may be able to fake it if it suits their goals, but they do not have real empathy at all. Other humans are just there to provide something of value to the psychopath. If the psychopath sees that something bad is happening to another person, he will just wonder how this affects him/her or could use that to his/her advantage. It would never be a feeling of empathy towards that person.

Narcissistic Actions

An early sign that can show up with a narcissist is fantasies and even daydreams about immense status and power levels. Many narcissists will report that they had fantasies of being adored and worshipped even when they were children. While many non-narcissistic people may have this kind of daydream on occasion, they will feel that they deserve this elevation and praise because it is their basic right. And the fact that there are times when they are not being revered or worshipped is seen as a personal affront to these people.

They believe that the statement, "I am better than most people. They are not worthy of me. I am above them." is something that most narcissists will feel. Yes, there are times when humans are going to have an inflated sense of self- image, such as after a significant achievement. But a narcissist will view praise and flattery as something that they should get all of the time, no matter what circumstances are going on around them.

The inflated sense of self-worth that the narcissist experiences internally can show up outwardly as well. This can show up in two ways. They will always need praise and agreement, and they will despise any form of rejection or criticism. The approval of others and all of the praise are like oxygen to the narcissist's ego, and they just cannot function without it. Things might get ugly if the people around them aren't complimenting the narcissist.

An example of this is a dictator who is in a hermit state. These people will demand worship from those over whom they have control, asking that statues be built in their likeness in exchange for complete acceptance and obedience. When one of the people disagrees or commits an act of dissent, they will be punished harshly and quickly.

Sadism

Sadism may not be one of the Dark Triad aspects, but it is still something necessary to add to this. Modern researchers into psychology have proposed that the Dark Triad is composed of four parts and that a sadistic personality disorder should be added to this. Sadism is sometimes the hardest personality trait to understand because it is often the least relatable out of all of them. Sadism is when the person derives some sort of pleasure from the suffering of others. This could add a new and worrying dimension to the preexisting traits that we have conferred above. They would not be sorry if the Machiavellian leader wished to make others suffer. If somebody were a sadist, though, they would relish the pain. They would take pleasure in the heinous atrocities that take place.

The feature that will set sadism apart from some of the other aspects of dark psychology is that it is all about cruelty. This cruelty is just there to please the one using it. It is not there to serve a larger purpose. It is not there to give the manipulator any control. Sadists are only interested in inflicting pain on others because it is amusing to them, and they like seeing it.

THE INTERNET AND DARK PSYCHOLOGY

Psychology is a science that encompasses the study of human thoughts, behaviour, emotions, and the mind. The beautiful thing is when one gets a deeper understanding of how psychology operates, it can significantly benefit ourselves and our everyday interactions with others. Man is a social being – therefore, it must process social behaviours that psychology seeks to understand, usually explains, and sometimes predicts.

A large part of psychology aims to diagnose and treat mentally derailed individuals who possess a threat to the general public.

Psychology is all around you – your everyday activity, and your interaction with others, that TV commercial you saw recently, the print ads, the website you are most frequently on, and so on.

Interestingly, there is psychology involved in any human problem, no matter the age or gender, and psychologists aim to make life better and improve human behaviour. Part of this, as we know, involves looking at the darker side of human nature.

Dark psychology aims to understand the various thoughts, reasoning, perception, or feelings that often lead to human predatory behaviour that leads to the inhumane and brutal victimization of others without any reasonable human comprehension.

Internet trolls can also be an agent of destruction. An Internet troll starts a quarrel and offends people online. According to psychology, such people may have dark personality traits. They live a life based on their sadistic nature, and others must suffer the same fate – they naturally make you feel bad. Most times, there is a psychological disorder triggered by experience or an ongoing occurrence. When you encounter a troll, the best thing to do is completely ignore them as they feed on your suffering, which gives them great pleasure.

These internet trolls can be called predators. These people are first-class cyberbullies, stalkers, criminals, sexual predators, and the like. They use the power of the Internet to gather useful information about their victims or targets.

A predator can be a group of people or persons that, directly or indirectly, enjoys stalking, exploring, and victimizing unsuspecting individuals by using the power of information communication technology (ICT). They are often consumed with their desire for power, fantasies, or just suffering from loneliness and searching for acceptance. A predator can be of any age, gender, or economic status. Once upon a time, all we had to deal with were human predators. But with the rise of the technological age, things are now even more complicated as predators harness ICT's power and use it to their advantage – creating profiles and becoming almost untraceable.

Dark Traits and Online Activities

The Internet is a world of its own. It is a chain of networks communicating with billions of other systems. You have access to almost anything you can think of. Despite having wonderful advantages, the disadvantages can be life- threatening. One of the common disadvantages is that people who spend a lot of time working in front of a computer often get ill. They get weaker, develop eye issues, back pain, and so on. Some people develop addictions, some fall into depression, and suffer from serious health issues, while many end up with serious social issues or psychological disorders.

The Internet takes the different behaviours and activities we engage in offline and makes them practical online as well. Imagine someone addicted to sex, games, or shopping. When such a person gets online, it becomes unlimited, which later turns into a habit. If the Internet has such an effect on the average person, imagine what dangers it would pose in the hands of a predator. Narcissists are proud and lack empathy. Machiavellians are manipulative and lack morals, while psychopaths are selfish and remorseless.

Categorically, the dark personality triad is a big influence on the behaviours of predators that troll online. The online behaviour of a psychopath can be remorseless while a Machiavellian manipulates, and a narcissist is preoccupied with getting attention. With all of these traits in mind, one can easily pinpoint an internet troll that possesses a dark personality. Several researchers discovered that dark personality triad behaviours are mostly found on their social media platforms like Facebook. Most trolls have a psychopathic tendency and promote themselves or their social status using social media platforms.

Because he/she is proud, his/her online activity is a demonstration of superiority, as evidenced by the photographs he/she uploads that demonstrate his/her money and success. They can be greedy and arrogant, or they can be domineering and driven by a desire for power and status. Machiavellians, on the other hand, seek to manipulate and deceive unknowing victims to achieve their own goals. The psychopath, in their way, is the most destructive of all the three personalities.

The psychopath has no conscience, is violent, and very aggressive. Hypothetically speaking, psychopathy in the form of trolling is more frequent among popular people on Facebook. On the other hand, a narcissist might not be a troll but will see themselves as superior to everyone. They look down on people, and they believe that they are special. Psychopathic traits can be sadistic, and they may find pleasure in harming others for fun's sake. So, it is acceptable to say that abnormal online behaviour is mostly psychopaths.

HOW NOT TO BE MANIPULATED

How To Defend Yourself from Manipulators

We are, at the end of the day, humans. It is precise because of this that we can focus on other people's perspectives in whatever we do. We crave and enjoy receiving validation from others so that we may make an unconscious decision about whether or not we will be depressed. The norm in the millennial era has been to brag about their money on social media. Many of these braggings are often the reality but in the end, this leads to a loose connection with reality. This kind of self-deception can penetrate the human system to the point that a victim may one day wake up and realize that her beautiful environment only exists in her servant's mind. Depression will closely follow suit. The first step towards protecting yourself against persuasion and manipulation is to confront the scenario and to take the position of disrupting any illusions. You will not be able to live your lives normally. You must exercise caution in regulating your own decisions and then deciding to perceive things for what they truly are. This deal, which appears to be too good to be true, may be true. Another thing you should do is to trust your gut impulses. Sometimes you have been told a lie in the most professional manner possible. But at a specific instinctive rate, you can feel an imbalance between what should, what is, and then what is projected on you. There might be no physical sign that something is wrong, but you think that something is wrong. The next significant thing when you ask questions is to hear the answers. This can sound unbelievable because you are going to listen to the responses. The reality is that we can deceive ourselves by choosing the responses we receive. We say that we look, but we only care about the reactions that we want to hear and not the answers that we receive. Although you may have broken your illusions, some of you still cling to their comfort. Because of the suffering that comes with dealing with the situation, you would not get genuine answers to your inquiries. Actual hearing needs a sense of detachment, but that is not the case this time.

You must get rid of your feelings. Your detachment from your emotions would lead you to the next step in processing the new data logically. It can make situations more complicated than they have to be. It makes it so hard for your exit strategy, to allow all feelings to cool down and spring. The irrational part of you may want to let everything go to hell when you face reality. Your justified anger can encourage you to take short-term measures to calm your feelings. But you may come to regret these actions in the long term. This does not mean that you should deny your emotions, but it also does not mean that you should not act on these emotions. First, deal with the situation and later deal with your emotions.

Act Fast

It is wonderful that you have come to terms with the truth. But defending ourselves against this evil, deceitful method entails so much more. It is frequently intense and exciting at first as you struggle to protect yourself from the claws of these manipulators. The intensity of these emotions can lead to negation over time. The longer you take any action, the quicker the denial will begin – and if it occurs, there is a strong likelihood that you may fall back and end up being trapped on the same internet. You can avoid this by taking action as soon as you know someone is attempting to manipulate you. This can be done in the most natural way possible, such as informing a close friend about details of a specific incident. This will set in motion all of the events that will finally lead to your liberation. You should understand that after choosing to behave, the fabric is made of sturdier material than glass. The illusion can work its way back to your core by using fragmented parts of your feelings to solve it. When a liar is caught, they may try to have others carry out the deception if they believe they no longer have you in their sights. A disgruntled partner with whom you have recently had problems would try to persuade you to rethink your opinion by using the other shared linkages in your lives. If you want to come out of this alive, you will need to use both your reasoning and your instincts. While the reality is that discovering you have always been lied to leaves you emotionally traumatized, you are nevertheless unaffected by the situation. Priority should be given to following the path that will allow you to reach this poisonous condition without causing further harm. Mentally, you are all over the place. Rage, hurt, and disappointment is the tip of the iceberg. But you must logically believe. Keep your head above the water and warn yourself.

Get Assistance Quickly

When you are trapped in the manipulations of others, confusion is one of the feelings you would encounter. This will obscure your rational thinking and make you feel helpless. You could even question the truth of what you are currently facing. If you continue to have those doubts, it will lead to denial. You will likely want to say that you have the whole scenario wrong. You misunderstood specific stuff and came to the incorrect conclusion. Such thinking would lead back to the weapons of the manipulator. Resist the desire to accept a second opinion. In a health crisis, people go to another physician to get a second view. This is to clear any doubts about your first diagnosis and to confirm the best course of therapy for you.

Similarly, receiving an opinion from another person can assist you in discerning reality and your next steps. Just remember, it is better to go to someone who has proven to have your best interest at heart. The next step is to confront the perpetrator if you have the assistance that you need. It is recommended that you choose the scene or place for this. Select a location that provides you the upper hand. That would involve some cautious planning on your part. If the offender exists in the cyber world, especially if you have been swindled by the person, you must engage the police and the authorities concerned. Do some of your research to find out the truth. After you face the offender and take the measures you need to get out of the scenario, the healing method must begin rapidly. The extent and severity you have been harmed, manipulated, or abused do not matter. You have to be able to go through it and wait for your wounds to be "healed", rather than sitting on your bed and living the past.

Although time would provide you with enough distance from your experience, you would rarely be able to cure emotional scars if you learned something from this book. If you do not act, an unhealthy scab will form over the wound, making you just as vulnerable as you were before. Speak to a consultant, take part in the treatment, and actively facilitate the healing process, regardless of what you choose. It will not occur overnight, but you are sure you get nearer each day with every phase of your treatment.

Your Instincts

While your brain interprets signals based on facts, logic, and experience, it operates in the opposite direction by filtering data through an emotional filter. The only thing that takes vibrations is your intestine that cannot pick up either the heart or the brain. You will be less likely to be tempted by others who try to manipulate you if you can cultivate yourself to the point where you recognize and train your inner voice. It is difficult to acknowledge this voice at first, and this is because we have permitted sounds of doubt, self- discrimination, and the loud voices of the critics within and without drowning our authentic voices in our lives. This voice or instinct relies on your survival. So, trust that your brain cells will still be able to process stuff in your immediate area when it starts. Some individuals call it intuition, some call it instinct – and they do the same, particularly when it comes to relationships. You must acknowledge that starting to trust your instincts may not always make logical sense. If you have ever been doing something and felt like you were suddenly watched, then you understand what this means.

You have no eyes at the back of your head, no one else in the room, but a slight shiver runs down the back of your neck, and you are gazing at the "sudden understanding," which is exactly what is being discussed. The first step in connecting with your instinct is to decode your mind with your voices. You can do this with meditation. Forget about conversing and focus on your core. You are the voice that you recognize. After then, pay attention to your thoughts. Do not toss your head's eclectic monologues out the window. Rather, go with the flow of your thoughts.

Why do you believe in somebody somehow? How do you feel so deeply, even though you knew each other for only a few days? What's this nagging feeling about this other individual? You become more sensitive to your intuition as you explore your ideas and know when your instincts start and respond to them. You might have to learn to stop and believe if you are the individual who, at present, wants to make stimulating choices. This break provides you the chance to reflect and assess your options. The next part is hard, and many people cannot follow it. You cannot sail or navigate this step, unfortunately. You need to be open to the concept of self-confidence and trusting others to believe in your instinct. Your lack of confidence would only make you paranoid, and when you are paranoid, it is not your instincts that kick. It is your fear! Fear tends to turn into a mountain from a molehill. You must let go of your fears, embrace trust, and take control of your new relationships. Without the mental blockages of fear, you can hear the voice more clearly. Finally, you must reevaluate your priorities.

If money and worldly possessions are at the forefront of your consciousness, you may not be able to see the past. Any contact you have with people will be seen as somebody trying to take advantage of you, and this will quickly become the fact if you live like this all of the time. Let us be clear – we bring what we believe in into your lives. If you always think about material wealth, you will only attract individuals like yourself. Look at your interactions with this new view with this guide – the old, the new, and the outlook. Do not enter into a partnership you expect to play. Be accessible to them, whether it is a business relationship, a romantic relationship, or just a regular acquaintance. You can receive the correct feedback from your intuition. Do not believe that if you come across suspects, your gut instinct would advise you to turn around.

CONCLUSION

Thank you for reading this book.

Reading people is a very important skill for anybody to have. This is because it will allow you to understand the complete message somebody is passing across when you are having a conversation with said person. This will put you ahead in your dealings with people and help establish you as a force to reckon with. Humans for a fact say more nonverbally than they do verbally which is why if you are to truly grasp what someone is communicating, you should be able to read and understand their nonverbal communication.

Listening to nonverbal communication is an art that requires training to develop. This particular means of communication, as you now know, says and hints at much more than you are liable to hear and get from having an oral or written conversation with somebody. For instance, body movement can be used to communicate a message in four different ways.

Being adept at the art of nonverbal communication requires that you master some five principles. These principles will not only allow you to identify nonverbal cues but will also help interpret them correctly. Without mastery of these principles, you will be prone to make mistakes where reading people is concerned.

Being a master nonverbal communicator also requires that you constantly work on yourself. When you look at things from a different perspective, it becomes easier to understand and look beyond appearances.

Good luck.